GW00746040

A. Mark Thomas was born at the Entrance, New South Wales, in 1959. He attended Monash University, Victoria, graduating with a Bachelor of Arts degree in English and American Literature and American History. He also read law at the University of Tasmania, 1981–83.

He is currently the sports news editor for the *Examiner* in Launceston, Tasmania, where he lives with his wife.

ACKNOWLEDGEMENTS

The author would like to thank the following for kindly contributing to this book: Allan Border, Dean Jones, Geoff Marsh, Mike Gatting, Sir Richard Hadlee, Neville Oliver; Rick Finlay for statistical information; Gregg Porteus, Darren Tindale, John Barnes, Graham Morris, and Nikhil Bhattacharya for photographs (and photographic staff from Australia's major newspapers); and the *Examiner* for use of its computer system.

BOON: IN THE FIRING LINE

An Autobiography with A. Mark Thomas

SUN
AUSTRALIA

I dedicate this book to my late father, Clarrie Boon, and especially to my wife, Pip, and children, Georgina and Jack.

A. Mark Thomas dedicates this work to his wife, Kathryn. And his parents, Max and Elaine Thomas, sister Helen, and brother Greg.

First published 1993 by Pan Macmillan Publishers Australia, a division of Pan Macmillan Australia Pty Limited 63–71 Balfour Street, Chippendale, Sydney. A.C.N. 001 184 014

Copyright © DPB Enterprise Pty Ltd. 1993

All rights reserved. No part of this book may be reproduced or transmitted in any form or by any means, electronic or mechanical, including photocopying, recording or by any information storage and retrieval system, without prior permission in writing from the publisher.

National Library of Australia cataloguing-in-publication data:

Boon, David.
Boon: in the firing line.

ISBN 0 7251 0724 3.

1. Boon, David. 2. Cricket players – Tasmania – Biography. 3. Cricket players – Australia – Biography. I. Thomas, A. Mark. II. Title.

796.358092

Typeset in 11/16 pt Cheltenham by Midland Typesetters, Maryborough
Printed by Australian Print Group, Maryborough, Australia

CONTENTS

FOREWORD

If you did a poll among world cricketers as to whom you would like to have out in the middle batting for your life, David Boon would rank very highly on the list. He has established himself over the last ten years as a premier batsman in all conditions, against all types of bowling. He is a man for all seasons, someone you can depend upon in any situation.

David has played some fantastic innings for Tasmania and Australia; the ones that stick in my mind most are three of his four Test centuries at the Sydney Cricket Ground. First, against England in the Bicentenary Test, then against the West Indies and, more recently, against India.

I believe that right from an early age, David has been thrust into a position of scoring heavily for his side or see that team crumble. This has made him into the fierce and fine competitor we see today.

David came into the Australian side during our rebuilding period, when the team struggled for a few seasons. Through that time, he was as solid as the Rock of Gibraltar, on and off the field, and a tremendous ally to me personally.

Boonie is a man after my own heart: he enjoys a beer and chat and it is not unusual to see Border and Boon perched at a bar, or, in fact, still in our whites enjoying a cold beer doing a post mortem of the day's events.

David is a quiet achiever, a person who never has a bad word to say about anyone and, in fact, there are times out in the field that he's that quiet, especially under the helmet at short leg, someone has always got to belt him to make sure he's still awake.

In this book, David gives the reader a great insight into his life behind the scenes and makes you more aware of what a great bloke we have in the 5′2″ Tasmanian with the flared pants.

May there be many more runs from the Keg on Legs.

Well done, Babs.

Allan Border

INTRODUCTION

At a gala dinner in December 1989 to celebrate Tasmania's first Test match – Australia versus Sri Lanka – Richie Benaud stepped onto the podium. In front of Benaud, in the ballroom of the Sheraton Hobart Hotel, sat the two teams, most of the Australian Cricket Board's hierarchy and 500 guests.

The assembled audience had witnessed a video-film of the history of Tasmanian cricket, one which – strangely – failed to highlight David Boon's considerable achievements. Benaud took it upon himself to do just that. He likened Boon to the former England batsman Ken Barrington who 'used to walk onto the ground like he had a Union Jack draped around his shoulders'.

'There's something about him that tells you Boonie's tough,' Benaud said. 'David doesn't say a great deal, but when he walks out to play in the baggy green cap of Australia, there have been players who have been just as proud, but no one more proud, to play for Australia.'

Former Australian skipper Greg Chappell once wrote that Boon was one cricketer who had had to work harder than his counterparts. Chappell's theory was that Boon grew up batting on inferior wickets and facilities, as opposed to the larger mainland states.

Boon's supporters also lacked the political clout available to other states, all of which possess powerful media voices and influential ex-Test players (which Tasmania has never had), who have a natural and traditional avenue to the Australian selection process.

However, ABC cricket commentator Neville Oliver sees things differently. For him, Boon was always under the eye of selectors because he was so obviously the greatest talent in Tasmania, from the time he was first selected for the Australian Under-19 team as a 16-year-old to tour England in 1977.

Boon the person is somewhat of an enigma: publicly the 'strong, silent type'; privately – within a close but large circle of family and team-mates – a rare wit; but more importantly, a man of enormous compassion and understanding.

Boon is not a saint. But he has worked very hard at the gifts God bestowed upon him, to overcome adversity, and prosper – while making an extraordinary number of friends and having a good time along the way.

My own relationship with Boon began when I first came to work as a journalist with the *Examiner* newspaper in Launceston, Tasmania, in 1984. I was a reporter, even in those early days concentrating on sport. David was Tasmania's star cricketer, seemingly pre-destined for the Australian Test team.

Being Tasmanian based, I have witnessed most of Boon's Test innings via the television, so I haven't been able to see Boon first-hand after major success or failure. Usually, we speak on the telephone, collaborating in a weekly (sometimes tri-weekly) newspaper column through the cricket season and on major overseas tours.

During our association, I have developed a number of rules when compiling David's column: first, asking Boon about the depth or breadth of a personal innings is like pulling impacted wisdom teeth; second, he will praise team-mates and opponents alike for good performances; third, controversial statements or criticism are not part of Boon's style.

My first major story about Boon was on his selection for the Ashes tour of 1985, after his first domestic season with the Test team, playing against the West Indies. I covered Boon's dropping from the Australian team in 1986–87, when he returned home from the America's Cup Challenge one-day series. He was understandably disappointed and disheartened, but he was full of desire to return to the national team.

This was probably Boon's lowest ebb. In the next Sheffield Shield match against Queensland, Boon faced his long-time friend Craig McDermott – and was caught by Glenn Trimble off the glove for three. After the day's play, Boon – for the first and only time – refused to speak with me as a member of the press. He went home and decided to chop wood in a bid to relieve his frustration. Instead, he suffered an injured hand during this chore.

It was during this time that Boon had happened upon Sir Garfield Sobers' comment that a batsman 'isn't at rock-bottom until he admits that he's there'. Nursing a bruised hand, his ego in tatters, his Australian vice-captaincy lost with his Test place, Boon decided that the descent to rock-bottom had been made.

In the second innings of that Shield game against Queensland, Boon made 172 and saved Tasmania from any chance of outright defeat. Make no mistake, this period of Boon's life was his watershed – when he had to make up his mind whether to continue at his chosen level or retreat to the Sheffield Shield competition and enjoy the occasional foray into the international arena.

Boon had played twenty-three Test matches when he was dropped in 1986–87, a reasonable contribution by some standards. But not the parameters set by Boon. He weathered the controversy surrounding his suspension from the Tasmanian team for 'disciplinary reasons' after an incident in a Hobart hotel in early 1987. And came back. He was player of the series in the Sharjah one-day tournament and at the 1987 World Cup won four Man of the Match awards, including the one in the final.

Boon's toughness is legendary, a person capable of enduring much more than a Test batsman's usual litany of broken fingers and livid body parts. In November, 1989, Australia played New Zealand in the first Test match at the WACA Ground in Perth, Western Australia. Boon made 200, his highest Test score. However, at the

start of the summer, Boon had wrenched his left knee fielding in
the deep in a one-day match against Western Australia on the same
ground. On the last day of the Test – which Mark Greatbatch saved
for New Zealand – Boon damaged the knee again, diving for a catch
at bat-pad, the position in which he is regarded as one of the world's
best.

Rather than come off the field of play, Boon struggled to his
feet and hunched over again. He kept diving for chances and his
knee just got worse and worse. Some might say his actions were
ill-considered – a fit 12th man would have been a better proposition.
But Boon, particularly with a Test victory on the line, would have
had to have been incapable of standing before he would have
relinquished his spot.

He missed Tasmania's next Sheffield Shield match against Victoria
in Launceston. But he returned to play in that historic Test match
against Sri Lanka at Bellerive Oval, leading Australia out onto the
ground with his opening partner Mark Taylor (Geoff Marsh had
suffered a broken toe at a Test net in Perth). Boon made 41 in
the first innings. Before Australia's second outing, Boon hurt his
knee again in a fielding drill.

Then Australian and Tasmanian paceman Greg Campbell hit the
injured joint with a net delivery! Boon hobbled out with a runner
for the second innings. But the first delivery he received from Graeme
Labrooy, Boon smash-cut the ball off the meat of the bat – straight
to Rumesh Ratnayake in the gully.

Boon is also very much aware of his responsibilities at home
in Tasmania, when the focus of his 'fishbowl' existence is increased
at least five-fold. He is rarely too busy, too tired or uninterested
to sign an autograph for a fan or have a chat.

His relationship with children, whether at a game, in the street
or a cricket clinic, is remarkable. The ones who stand open-mouthed,
gaping at their hero are greeted warmly, as Boon tries to first break
the ice, or if that is impossible, patted on the back and blessed
with Australia's ubiquitous 'G'day, mate!' to make their day.

Boon is, in many ways, an old-fashioned, conservative man. He believes in being loyal to people and expects similar loyalty in return. One of Boon's oft-repeated descriptions is that so-and-so is a 'good bloke'. Boon himself is a good bloke. But he is much more than that. He is a good person and a good friend.

1
THE
BEGINNING

A small, dark-headed boy is running downfield, a hockey stick gripped in his hands. At the end of the stick, as if attached by a thread, is a hockey ball. The boy dribbles the ball from one end of the field to the other, never losing control. It is the early 1960s. The boy is three years old.

He stops and turns to wave to his mother, who plays club hockey in Launceston, Tasmania. The boy raises his hockey stick towards his family. His name is David Clarence Boon.

In the 1992–93 Australian domestic cricket season, Boon raised his bat to the players' viewing area at the 'Gabba ground in Brisbane. He was acknowledging a Test century – his fourteenth – first to his Australian team-mates, then to the cricketing public. The previous summer, Boon had scored three centuries against India – in Sydney, Adelaide and Perth.

In 1992–93, Australia was defeated 2–1 by the West Indies in an engrossing contest between the two cricket nations. For the first time in a Test series since 1975–76, Australia came within two runs of beating the cricketers from the Caribbean . They were principally denied by the West Indies' paceman Curtly Ambrose whose record-equalling haul of wickets – 33 in a series – matched that of Clarrie Grimmett and Alan Davidson.

David Boon finished the season with 490 runs at an average of 61.25, topping both the Australian average and aggregate tables. In fact, he was the leading run-scorer of both countries for the five-Test series. The next best was West Indian left-hander Brian Lara, who made 466 at 58.25, including his maiden century, a magnificent 277 at the Sydney Cricket Ground.

In the second Test in Melbourne, Boon surpassed Australian coach and former Australian captain Bob Simpson on the Australian all-time run-scoring list. In the second Test in Wellington on the 1993 tour of New Zealand, Boon overtook another Australian captain, Bill Lawry, to become Australia's seventh-highest batsman. At the end of the 1993 New Zealand tour, Boon had scored 5314 runs at an average of 43.91, which included the 14 centuries and 25 half-centuries. Crucially, Boon was just behind Ian Chappell (5345 runs) and Doug Walters (5357) as he started the Ashes tour of England in '93.

Of his 14 hundreds, Boon has scored six against India, three against both England and West Indies and two against New Zealand, including his highest Test score of 200 in Perth, 1989-90.

When Boon scored 129 not out at the Sydney Cricket Ground in '91–92, it was his fourth century on that arena – equalling the feats of Greg Chappell and Englishman Walter Hammond. By scoring 135 in the Test at the Adelaide Oval in that season, he became the only person to notch up four centuries at that ground, an achievement Sir Donald Bradman never made.

David Boon started as a middle-order batsman, went to number three and then forged, with Geoff Marsh, Australia's best opening partnership since Bob Simpson and Lawry were together. After batting at number three for two years, Boon was recalled to the opener's spot to partner Mark Taylor against West Indies and New Zealand. For the following tour of England, however, his captain Allan Border stated that Boon would return to number three against England.

Boon's cricket career and achievements will be forever linked with Tasmanian cricket, for which he has been the instantly recognisable public face since he made his way to the wicket for the second Test match against the West Indies at the 'Gabba in Brisbane in 1984–85.

Boon was then twenty-four. But his name was first mentioned in a national context when, aged 16, he scored a century for an Australian Schoolboys XI at the Melbourne Cricket Ground. He batted at nine, a late inclusion when a South Australian batsman – Brian Mitchell – was seconded to the opposing Australian Cricket Board team.

Boon was subsequently selected in the Australian Under-19 team which toured England in 1977, as part of the Queen's Silver Jubilee celebrations. That team also included Geoff Marsh, Wayne Phillips and Greg Dwyer. But only Boon had survived at Test level by the end of 1992–93, after his best mate Marsh was dropped the previous summer.

In 1978, Boon scored the winning runs for Tasmania in a Gillette Cup one-day semi-final against Queensland – hitting the second-last delivery of the match from former Test bowler Phil Carlson to the boundary. Boon was seventeen years old.

His long-time mentor was Jack Simmons, the Lancashire spinner who came to Tasmania to coach the Northern Tasmanian Cricket Association. Simmons discovered Boon as a 10-year-old, at the Charles Street Primary School, a right-hander blessed with the necessary hand-eye co-ordination, a natural technique, and the ability to play straight.

However, Boon's story isn't one of a child prodigy developing into an Australian cricketing hero. There have been many pitfalls along the way. Boon made his Sheffield Shield debut in 1978, the game after the Gillette Cup win, but his first Test cap eluded him until the second match against the West Indies at the 'Gabba in 1984–85. Until then he had only been picked for one limited-overs international the season before.

From 1979–82, Tasmania played only five Sheffield Shield matches a season in a restricted format. In the season of 1982–83, Tasmania earnt full Shield 'rights'. In Boon's third season Shield cricket, he made his first century, 114 against Victoria at the TCA Ground in Hobart in December 1980.

In his first Test season, Boon played three matches and scored a total of 132 in five innings at an average of 26.40. His highest score, 51, came in the second innings of his debut Test. He was selected for the Ashes tour of England in 1985, but was found wanting against spin at Test level, as 124 runs at 17.17 testifies.

Test series against New Zealand and India in Australia, New Zealand in New Zealand and India in India followed between 1985–86. However, Boon's watershed season came in 1986–87, when England came to Australia to begin again the Ashes contest. Boon played the first four Test matches of the series, scoring only 144 runs in eight innings – including 103 at the Adelaide Oval – for an average of 18.00.

He was dropped from the Australian team for the fifth and final Test match in Sydney, losing the vice-captaincy of the national XI. There was worse to come. Boon played against Queensland at the NTCA Ground in Launceston, followed by a match against New South Wales at the TCA Ground. Boon, who was Tasmanian captain at the time, and Shield team-mates Glenn Hughes, the younger brother of former Australian captain Kim, were suspended for one match after an alleged incident which occurred in the evening of the first day of the Hobart match.

However, despite the suspension – 'disciplinary reasons' was the then Tasmanian Cricket Council's only official comment – Boon was retained in the Australian squad which played in the Sharjah limited-overs tournament in March 1987. There he was named man of the series, scoring three successive half-centuries. But upon returning to Tasmania, the TCC announced that former State skipper Brian Davison was in the job at the expense of Boon.

It was at this moment, for the second time in his career, that Boon pondered leaving his home state. But he remained.

Boon then went to India for the 1987 World Cup. History shows that Australia won the Cup and Boon chalked up four Man-of-the-Match awards, including one in the final against England.

Boon then faced another nemesis and former Tasmanian team-mate, Sir Richard Hadlee, in the Test series against New Zealand in Australia in 1987–88. In the first Test at the 'Gabba in Brisbane, Boon scored 143, making a total of 237 runs at an average of 47.40 in five innings.

The Bicentennial Test match against England at the Sydney Cricket Ground followed. Boon made 184 not out in the second innings and saved the match for Australia. It was here in Sydney, having driven himself incessantly in net sessions, that Boon demonstrated his mastery of spin bowling, particularly over John Emburey.

It was also in this season that Boon was voted International Cricketer of the Year.

EARLY BOON

David Boon was born on 29 December 1960, the first of two children to his parents, Clarrie and Lesley.

The Boons were married in 1958 in Launceston's Anglican St John's Church. Clarrie Boon was a newsagent, and his foresight and diligence provided the vast majority of factual data for this publication. Lesley Boon is a former national hockey player; in fact, she was the Australian vice-captain in 1958–59.

The pair described their son as an ordinary, active child, albeit one who was adept at ball games from an early age. The Boons suffered more than the regulation number of broken windows from cricket balls and footballs.

However, young David was also a hazard to himself, a lad whose hairline hides a multitude of scars from various wounds. His trademark moustache hides a major scar, achieved by catapulting himself out of the family car and into the kerbside.

'He pulled the stitches out that night!' remembered Mr Boon.

'Just a rusher,' Mrs Boon stated. 'He just went at everything when he was a little boy. He was a full-going concern physically, not talkatively. He didn't do much talking; he did much action. He would just go where angels feared to tread.'

David's co-ordination was developed early, as his hockey skills at aged three demonstrated. His parents said that David as a young boy, in physical terms, is closely matched by his first child, daughter Georgina, who already shares her father's extraordinary eye-hand co-ordination. She was able to repeatedly strike soft tennis balls, thrown by her father, with a junior racquet when she was three.

Mrs Boon began David's foot co-ordination with a soccer ball – not the code preferred by Mr Boon, who played Australian football with North Launceston and East Launceston in the former Northern Tasmanian Football Association in the 1950s.

'He was quite good at those sorts of things; he would concentrate,' Mrs Boon said. 'But Clarrie was horrified! He came home and said, "What on earth are you doing? You haven't got an Australian Rules football. Whatever are you teaching him?" I said he might be an international soccer player. Who wants to play AFL when you can play soccer, soccer being one of my passions.'

David's first organised sporting activity was swimming. However, the way he came to be involved highlights one of the major parts of his psychological make-up – his shyness.

As an eight-year-old David was introduced to swimming, like most young Australians, in a 'Learn to Swim' program. One afternoon, at the Windmill Hill swimming centre in Launceston, David was watching South Esk Swimming Club members go through their paces. The South Esk coach, Ross Smith, approached and asked whether David would like to join in. Young Boon readily accepted the offer.

'That's typical David. He'd hang right back. Somebody had to invite him,' Mrs Boon said. 'He has always been like that. He's not a bit pushy. Next thing he said he'd like to join the club.'

So morning and night, Mr Boon would take David to training. He wasn't a champion swimmer, but Mrs Boon believes that he taught himself the difference between winning and losing. 'He organises himself. With swimming, we didn't have any push into that at all,' Mrs Boon said. 'He really did want to be part of it. David actually thrives on competing.

'The whole thing about swimming, which I think played a big part in his development, was that he wouldn't miss his training. He would put all his effort into it.

'Basically, the other boys were taller than David, with longer arms. He really had to work nine-pins against them. Because swimming's like that. But that didn't seem to deter him, it didn't seem to bother him. He just wanted be there competing. He'd make finals but he wouldn't be a medallist.

'You'd see other kids get out and they'd pout. Their mums would hurry down to them and say, never mind, darling. David would just pop out, grab his towel and be sitting there waiting for his next event.'

David's shyness almost stymied his early football career. He attended Charles Street Primary School, where Lancashire legend Jack Simmons first discovered Boon as a cricket prodigy. Boon was selected from Charles Street to attend the Northern Tasmanian football trials, which were being held at the East Launceston Primary School. A teacher at West Launceston, Peter Jones, a family friend, realised that David hadn't been on the field through the afternoon and asked why. 'Here was David sitting under a tree very quietly with the other boys,' Mrs Boon said. 'If Pete hadn't been there, and hadn't known about David, he would never have got into that team – he'd have still been sitting under the tree waiting to be called.' Boon was runner-up in the statewide primary school best and fairest award that year.

Mrs Boon shares with her son the experience and accompanying pressure of being recognised for her sporting prowess as a teenager – she was first selected to play hockey for Tasmania as 16-year-old Miss Lesley Sturzaker, her maiden name.

She had started playing hockey as an 11-year-old in Burnie, the city on the north-west coast of Tasmania. She played with the Old Darwinians club and was selected for the State trials in Launceston. It meant travelling away from home and staying in a hotel with the other North-West team members, a major excursion for a young woman attending Burnie High School in the early 1950s. Her mother's approval had to first be sought and gained.

'People in Burnie asked: "Weren't you even overcome with it?". I said I don't know why you're overcome with something at 16 when you're not even expecting it.'

She played in the national hockey carnival in South Australia in 1951 and won her first Australian blazer at the age of 20 in 1955. Mrs Boon said her development was a credit to her coaches – former Australian players Con Charlesworth and Meg Wilson, who is now the national president of women's hockey. 'Con Charlesworth was just about a legend in Australian hockey. She was in Australian teams and had been overseas a lot. I was very fortunate that she was Tasmanian coach at the time.'

Mrs Boon played for Australia in the International Conference – the forerunner of the world championships – in Sydney in 1956. 'Once I got in the Australian team, I had a thing that I had to stay there,' Mrs Boon said. 'I thought, over my dead body am I getting out of it! I think I stepped up my training and skills, because I just had this thing inside me that I wasn't getting out until I was good and ready.'

The 'good and ready' came in 1958, when Mr and Mrs Boon were married. Mrs Boon was again selected for the Australian team which went to the international conference in 1959, held in Holland – but she declined. Mrs Boon said that she regarded her life with Clarrie as just as important 'as any flipping hockey match!' And in 1960, David was born.

Mrs Boon returned to local hockey with the Penguins club in Launceston. However, with Mr Boon working from 4 am to 6 pm in the newsagent, she believed that raising David came before her state or national hockey ambitions. 'If you're at the stage where you're going to have children, well then, you take responsibility for them,' she said.

Mr Boon laughingly pointed out to his wife the psychological similarities between herself and their son. 'You can see where the determination comes from. From you!'

'I am quite determined about what you want to do,' Mrs Boon replied. 'It's the same as I say to David. You make up your own decisions on what life holds for you.'

Clarrie Boon was born in Launceston, but his family moved to the north-east of Tasmania, living in Scottsdale and Ringarooma, before he returned to his birthplace as a 14-year-old. He played A-Grade tennis as well as football, and kept wicket for Launceston High School – perhaps the origins of David's own sojourn behind the stumps when regular Australian gloveman Ian Healy was injured during the 1992 World Cup. After playing football with North Launceston and East Launceston, Clarrie became coach of the Brooks High School Old Boys amateur club in 1959. That was the beginning of his association with the Tasmanian Amateur Football League. He was president of the Northern League up until his death in February 1993.

David was about 14 when the influence of NTCA coach Jack Simmons ended his swimming career. Not that Simmons ordered young Boon out of the pool; David himself decided, through consultation with his parents, that cricket and training for the sport came first.

Simmons instigated the NTCA's first Under-13 Cricket Week in

1974 and Boon justified his early promise with a century and aggregate of 263 runs. David also took 23 wickets during the week!

Boon was 15 when first selected for the Tasmanian Under-19s in 1976, the national carnival held in Perth, Western Australia, in January, 1977. It was that same year that David came under the national spotlight. He was chosen as one of three Tasmanians – batsman David Hudson and spinner Chris Broadby were the other two – to go to Melbourne to play in a trial game foe selection for the first Australian Under-19 team to tour England that year.

Boon wasn't originally selected in Schoolboys XI, but replaced South Australian Bruce Mitchell, who was picked for the Australian Cricket Board team. Boon made 119, batting at number nine, and won a place in the touring party of 15, which went as part of the Queen's Silver Jubilee in 1977.

Boon was written up in the national newspapers and won his first 'poster' from the *Examiner* in Launceston – newsagents' hoardings bellowed Brilliant Century By Lton 16-Y-O.

But despite all the attention, Mr and Mrs Boon were adamant that David never had an over-inflated opinion of his abilities. 'I didn't feel that he ever did,' Mr Boon said. 'As far as home was concerned, I don't think he did. Basically, we had our feet too much on the ground.

'There were always further steps to go. I might say, "You haven't played senior football. You haven't reached what your mother reached." I never noticed anything, but I think we used to talk to him like that.' Mrs Boon agreed.

'If he was with me and anybody said, "Good on you, you were in the paper and you got a hundred," and they'd say to me, "He's going to a champion!" I'd to say, "Goodness me, you can be burnt out at 16!"

'You can classify anybody who's a good little tennis player, but it's a ridiculous statement to say they're going to be champion and they're going to play at Wimbledon. Some people are lovely club players. I said to David, when he got in the State team, we'll see how you go. As long as you try hard. If you try hard, you're not a disgrace. But if you don't try hard and give in, you're not much.

'There are some people who can be very good at State level but can't go up to international standard. If you can't, that's no disgrace to you. It's not your fault that you had talent but weren't quite able to step up.'

So Boon went to England in 1977 and the following summer, toured New Zealand as a member of the Tasmanian Under-19 team which played in an Australasian schoolboys tournament. Boon and Broadby, who also went on to play for Tasmania in the Sheffield Shield, were then selected to tour Sri Lanka with the Australian Under-19 team in February 1978. Upon their return, the pair started training again with the Tasmanian Sheffield Shield squad. However, when the opening Shield team was selected, Boon had to make himself unavailable because of his Higher School Certificate examinations at Launceston Church Grammar School.

That was also the year, 1978, that David was named captain of the Tasmanian Under-19s. However, the senior selectors decided to pick him for the next Sheffield Shield match against Queensland, which was preceded by a one-day Gillette Cup game.

For veteran Boon watchers, his reaction to the *Examiner*'s informing him of the start of his senior Tasmanian cricket career was classic Boon: 'Oh, that's good. Everyone has been saying I'd get in, but I didn't expect to. I wouldn't have been disappointed if I didn't make it because I've still got a few years yet.' As instructed by his mother Lesley, Boon had already become adept at never publicly discussing his possible selection until the team was officially named.

Boon and Gary Goodman, the former New South Welshman who came to Tasmania for cricket and made his home here, were the new State caps. Both starred on debut. Goodman made 100 exactly as an opener and was named Man of the Match; Boon, again batting at number nine, made 18 not out, including the winning four off the second last ball of the game at the 'Gabba.

The *Age*, the *Australian* (front page picture, Jack Simmons with a protective arm around Boon) and the Melbourne *Sun* responded with glowing reports. Queensland made 6–232; Tasmania responded with 9–236. Boon hit 10 runs from that last over – from Phil Carlson – to put Tasmania into the Gillette Cup final.

Six days later, Boon faced his first Shield game, coming to the wicket on a hat-trick, after Queensland paceman Dennis Schuller had dismissed Tasmanian vice-captain John Hampshire and wicketkeeper Roger Woolley, who would later precede Boon into the Australian Test team, with successive deliveries. Boon survived a bat-pad appeal first ball and was nought not out overnight. He went on to compile 22 runs on debut.

On 14 January 1979, Tasmania defeated Western Australia by 47 runs with five overs to spare at the TCA Ground in Hobart. Boon made eight runs during that memorable match; his mentor, Simmons, won the Man of the Match award by taking 4–17 from 10 overs.

Boon played against England, making 15 runs, in a one-day game at the NTCA Ground on 18 January 1979, and was relegated to twelfth man for the three-day match against the tourists at the TCA Ground.

Said England acting-captain Bob Willis after the one-dayer: 'Young Boon is a nice cut of a player certainly, but there's too much cockiness about him – he's too adventurous.'

In February that year, Boon was again selected for the Australian Under-19 team to play against Young England in a 'Mini-Test' and one-day international series.

In the winter of 1979, Boon again shelved his cricket gear temporarily to play football with North Launceston's Under-19s in the Northern Tasmanian Football Association. When North Launceston had four players selected in the Tasmanian team, Boon made his debut for the Robins, aged 18. A promising goal-kicking rover, Boon kicked three goals and North Launceston won the match.

However, a month later, Boon was suspended for four weeks on a striking charge in the Under-19s. Boon pleaded guilty at the tribunal. Basically, Boon had clobbered an opposing player who had been hitting a team-mate. This was David's last season of football because of cricket commitments and his first knee injury.

In Boon's first season of Sheffield Shield, he played two matches, three innings, made an aggregate of 34 runs with a top-score of 22.

During the period 1979–82, when Tasmania was restricted to only five Shield games a season – playing once against all the other States – Boon played every game. His first Shield century came in his third season, 114 – including 21 boundaries and a sixer – against Victoria at the TCA Ground in December 1980. Tasmanian captain Brian Davison made 173 batting at number five; the pair put on 174 for their fourth-wicket partnership.

Boon was first selected to play for Australia in a one-day match against the West Indies in 1983–84 and his Test debut came the following season.

However, while there has never been much doubt about Boon's cricket talents – first seen by Simmons when Boon was only 10 – his mental toughness, his ability to endure the inevitable hard times as an Australian cricketer come back to his early grounding.

'As far as we're concerned, David was absolutely normal. Never at any time did we treat him like he was special,' Mrs Boon said. 'We told him he had a gift and if he'd like to make use of it, he could, if he didn't want to, he didn't have to. We were more concerned that he learned how to lose and still hold his head up. I can't abide petulant people.'

2
TRIALS AND
TRIBULATIONS

TASMANIAN CAPTAINCY

David Boon captained Tasmania for three seasons, the first in 1984–85. Selected for the Prime Minister's XI to play the West Indies at Canberra's Manuka Oval, Boon celebrated with 134 runs. 'The TCC approached me about whether I'd like to be captain and I said yes,' Boon said.

He replaced Roger Woolley, the superbly talented middle-order right-hander, who preceded Boon as the first Tasmanian to be selected for Australia while a resident within the state. Woolley had won his Australian cap in the dual and difficult role of wicketkeeper-batsman.

Boon said that there was no animosity between himself and Woolley when he took up the captaincy. 'I looked at the position of captain in a positive manner,' Boon said. 'I thought, well, when you take on the captaincy, some are made for it, some aren't. The question of gaining respect of other people had never bothered me in the past.'

Previously, Boon had captained the Launceston Church Grammar School XI and been skipper of the Tasmanian Under-19s. The Under-19 tour of Sri Lanka, of which Boon was a member, was captained by Dirk Wellham, the former Test player who led New South Wales to two Sheffield Shields and captain-coached Tasmania in 1988–91.

In 1977, when the first Australian Under-19 schoolboy team, of which Boon was a 16-year-old member, went to England, Victorian Brad Green captained the squad.

When Boon took over the Tasmanian captaincy, Brian Davison – who later replaced Boon – had retired. The team's regular players were Woolley, Richard Soule (who took over the wicketkeeping role from the ex-captain), Mark Ray, Roger Brown, Roly Hyatt and Keith Bradshaw.

'I learnt a lot in that first year and thought I captained much better in the second,' Boon said. 'When you're a young guy captaining a side, there's a lot of input and conversation from your team-mates before any decision is made. But I have always advocated that as captain, the final decision is up to me. That means, if the team gets its bum kicked, it's on my head.

'But I also like to run a very open ship. Everyone has the right to provide input, to make a suggestion at any time or place. Once all the information is in, it's my job to say yea or nay, or stand by what I was going to do in the first place.'

Boon believes that earning respect as a captain comes from the right mix of on-field decisions and playing prowess. 'You earn the respect of the other guys not by setting yourself up on a pedestal. Your own performances have a lot to do with that, but if the other players have input, they also have to be involved all the time. Sometimes when you're captain, you can be thinking or concentrating on your own fielding and miss something. It's up to your team-mates to pick that up. It all comes back to being a good cricket team – you gain experience quickly if you think that way.'

Which reveals one of Boon's major cricket, even life, philosophies – the importance of the concept 'team'. 'In cricket, you can play an individual game within a team sport, but the bottom line is, the team is number one. If you all do your job well, then more often than not the team does well. I don't like cricketers who put making a century ahead of their team winning – they don't really care about losing.'

Obviously, Boon has based much of captaincy and cricket philosophy on the example of his Australian skipper, Allan Border. It is Border, among very few cricketers, who earns Boon's highest accolade. 'He's a guy for whom Australian cricket means everything. As a captain, he's very much open to suggestion. He quite often asks what the other guys think, not just his vice-captain. Although, he's been captain for a long time now and obviously knows what he wants to do, the Australian team always talks about the game plan the night before a match, a routine which we also use in Tasmania.

'It's up to everyone to perform their piece of the overall plan and if the team deviates, it's up to the captain to get everything back on the rails.'

Boon admits that Border can get annoyed, justifiably, when the elite of Australian cricket doesn't perform to its ability. 'But that can also be the responsibility of the team back-up, like Merv Hughes. You can hear him all over the MCG, lifting everyone through the quiet times. The captain knows that during a quiet session, you have to stick to your game plan. Eventually it's going to succeed, if you've done your homework right. If the plan doesn't work, it all comes back to the captain.'

Boon was replaced as captain at the beginning of the 1987–88, and his place taken by Brian Davison. At the end of that season, the talk was that Peter Faulkner, the all-rounder who played with Boon at Launceston Church Grammar School and the Launceston

Cricket Club, would be the new appointment. Davison, it was said, would act as coach-manager.

However, Australia's winter months – cricket's 'silly' season – saw the TCC have a major change of heart: Dirk Wellham was appointed as the captain-coach.

During Wellham's three seasons as captain, Tasmanian cricket certainly received an enormous boost in terms of publicity. Wellham has long been regarded as an astute leader, but also as a single-minded man.

In Wellham's first season, many Tasmanian fans were disgruntled with the sheer number of 'imports' in the Sheffield Shield team. Greg Shipperd, the former Western Australian opener who toured South Africa twice with Kim Hughes' rebels, and former Australian paceman David Gilbert, who had been a member of Wellham's winning Shield era in New South Wales were recruited along with talented all-rounder Rod Tucker, Gavin Robertson and Don O'Connor.

As a brief summary, Wellham's Tasmanian team challenged for a Shield final late into the season in both 1988–89 and 1989–90. However, the last summer was marred by the less-than-private differences of opinion between Wellham and the TCC.

Boon will not be drawn publicly on Wellham's performance, but admits honestly that they possess differing cricket philosophies. 'Dirk did a reasonable job captaining Tasmania and, at times, operated the unit very, very well. But not only the captain, the entire team didn't take full advantage of positive positions when they were in them. It's a hard thing to learn to go in for the kill. Tasmania got into quite a few situations where we could have won, but got scared of losing – you have to push home any advantage and ride it home.'

In Wellham's first year of captaincy, much Tasmanian media mileage was made of the fact that the team wasn't beaten outright. And there lies the difference between Boon and Wellham. 'My Sheffield Shield philosophy is, okay, we try and win as many as we can. If we lose a couple, that happens. Sheffield Shield cricket has got to become more exciting. You've got to try for results.

'There is an obvious "follow-on" situation in Australian cricket. You play club cricket to represent your State; you play State cricket to supply the Australian team – if you do that well, you will be a successful State. Players from New South Wales, Western Australia and Queensland have dominated within the Australian team since I started playing – and those three States have dominated the Sheffield Shield competition.'

Boon's philosophy is straightforward, but also backed by the mathematics of the Shield competition. 'If you play to win all the time, you might finish the season with four outright wins and two outright losses. You will get into the Sheffield Shield final because of the four wins, not because you lost two games.

'In Tasmania, we have got to concentrate for a period on trying to win. To improve, to become confident, we have got to play that way.'

Again, Boon's attitude to winning and captaincy comes back to the performances of Australia under the direction of Allan Border. 'Perhaps Dirk was influenced subconsciously by the desire not to get beaten. But that's Wellham's approach, not mine. I believe that when you get into a position to win, you go for it. It's more exciting for the players and supporters of cricket. It encourages players to stretch themselves to achieve their best possible performance.

'This attitude stems from a few good years I've experienced with Australia – we've started to play better and Allan Border's captaincy has helped. When we've got into a winning position, the thought of defeat has been non-existent. When we thought we could win, we went for it.'

Boon's primary example is obvious: Australia's victorious Ashes tour of England in 1989. After the fourth Test at Old Trafford, Australia was leading 3–0. 'We could have relaxed, the Ashes were ours. We could have lost the last two Tests and come home 3–2. But we said, "No way!". We were going to win the next two matches at Nottingham and Trent Bridge. And we would have won the last one if rain hadn't stopped us.'

For Boon, Border's aggressive captaincy was revealed with tactical ploys against England captain Graham Gooch in 1989 and Indian captain Mohammad Azharuddin in 1991–92. In England, Border would place himself at short mid-wicket and force Gooch to play in a manner, at that time, which was alien too him. So effective was that tactic, Gooch eventually excused himself from selection for England.

Boon himself became the means by which Azharuddin was foiled, Border positioning him at deep bat-pad. Boon is now regarded as one of the world's best close-in fieldsmen, and, even for his high standards, has taken some spectacular catches in that position.

However, Boon believes the difference between one captain and the next is playing personnel. 'There are great captains and there are others. But the great captains have always had good teams under them. Ian Chappell and Clive Lloyd were two of the best captains ever. They were very strong and committed within their own team, but you have to have a very good side to go with it . . . it makes the job that much easier.'

THE BOON–HUGHES INCIDENT

In March 1987, the third season of David Boon's first stint as Tasmanian captain, Tasmania played New South Wales in a Sheffield Shield game in Hobart. Tasmania batted and Boon and Glenn Hughes, who formed the opening pair, were dismissed. The Tasmanian team was staying at the Black Buffalo Hotel. 'Glenn and I had gone to Tattersalls (a Hobart restaurant-bar) for a meal and a couple of beers,' Boon recalls. 'I went back to our hotel about 10 o'clock to find a few of our boys playing cards – I decided to join the poker school. When Glenn joined the group, he and I ended up sitting next to each other.' It should be understood that Hughes has always been the Tasmanian team's scapegoat, especially for senior players such as Boon and former South Africa rebel all-rounder Peter Faulkner. In one memorable afternoon at the Bellerive Oval, several members of the media were summoned into the players' viewing area to find Hughes strapped to a medical stretcher with adhesive tape and begging for assistance.

Back at the Black Buffalo, Boon says that Hughes sat beside him, exposing hand after hand of cards. 'I kept saying, "Glenn, there's no use betting on those", and he was getting rather excited. He said, "You're looking at my hand, you cheating so-and-so!"' The game progressed, Hughes continuing to expose his cards and Boon, ever one to press home an advantage, keeping up the friendly abuse. 'Glenn finally said, "If you look at my cards again, I'm going to deck you". The next hand, he was holding his cards out in front of me and I told him there was no use betting on a pair of threes. He slapped me on the shoulder and I threw him on the bed and we wrestled around.'

The reaction to Boon's wrestling prowess was unsurprising – 'Glenn started squealing like a pig!' In the hubbub, Boon admits that an ashtray on an adjacent table was knocked to the floor and broken. However, the next day, Boon and Hughes were called before the Tasmanian coach-manager Graeme Mansfield, and Tasmanian Cricket Council chairman Mr Jack Bennett. The broken ashtray was mentioned and a charge of excessive noise was laid – along with the more serious 'crimes' of ripping a heater off a wall and breaking a table. Boon admitted and apologised for the possible disturbance to other guests in the hotel, while owning up that an ashtray may have been broken. Mr Bennett then suspended both Boon and Hughes for one match. 'I asked "Don't we get a chance to explain our side of the story?"' Boon said. 'We had our say, but Jack then said that the suspension still stood.'

There is no doubt that the Tasmanian administration, which had overseen the emergence of cricket from part-time to full-time

Sheffield Shield membership, was seeking to exert some major influence over its players. And there is no huge secret that the relationship between Boon as captain and Mansfield as coach could have been more productive. The upshot for Boon of the suspension was that headlines screamed around the country – first dropped as the vice-captain of the Australian team for lack of form, then as the Tasmanian captain suspended from his own Sheffield Shield side. The rumour-mill wasted no time: Boon and Hughes were accused of every possible variation of indiscretion. The affair even made the Tasmanian '7.30 Report'.

Boon and Hughes duly missed the next game against Western Australia in Perth. Boon has always admitted to the allegations of 'disturbing the peace', but has always emphatically denied the rest.

At the beginning of the next Australian season, with Boon safely back in the national team, his long-time Tasmanian team-mate and vice-captain Mark Ray wrote in the Melbourne *Herald* that the only thing Boon wasn't accused of was selling drugs. Perhaps the best off-the-cuff response again goes to David's wife, Pip, who when Boon returned home said, 'You can't have been suspended for only that – you must have thumped someone!' However, while Boon can see the humour in most situations after the event, he will never forget this particular black mark on his record, or those involved in it.

LOSING THE CAPTAINCY

Few people outside David Boon's inner circle will know how close Tasmania came to losing its favourite cricket son for the second time. Not for the goal of Australian Test or financial advancement – long feared to be the sole reason Boon would leave his beloved state of origin – but because of the way the Tasmanian cricket administration behaved when it dropped him from the captaincy for the 1987–88 season.

However, it came to pass that during the winter of 1987 Boon found himself sitting in the offices of the Victorian Cricket Association, opposite Ian Redpath and Ian 'Cocky' Chambers, discussing his cricketing future.

If we retreat a week or so, picture Boon working away in the marketing office of the then Tasmania Bank. Tasmanian Cricket Council chairman Jack Bennett telephones and asks Boon his thoughts on the captaincy. 'He said that some of the administration were concerned that there was perhaps too much responsibility on me,' Boon said. 'They had been discussing my Australian team commitments.

'I told him that I really enjoyed the Tasmanian captaincy and that I thought I had the respect of the other players. Over a period of time I had become more accustomed to the role of captain and I wanted to keep doing it. Jack said that he would discuss what I'd said with the other members of the board, and hung up.'

Five minutes later, Boon receives another telephone call, telling him to listen to the ABC Radio's next news bulletin. Boon does so, only to hear that the TCC had announced that he had been replaced by former skipper Brian Davison. 'That was on the 11 am bulletin and at 11.15, Jack Bennett rang back,' Boon said.

'He said that he'd rung around the available Board members and that, "We've all stood by our original decision and would like you to stand down."'

Before hanging up, Boon remembers saying, 'Thank you, Jack, I've already heard the news on the ABC!'

Boon's outward easy-going nature belies a man who believes in family, team-mates and friends. He is slow to anger, but when riled, his bad temper takes a similar time to diminish. When annoyed, one of his sayings is the ominous 'I've got a long memory'.

'I was really annoyed by the way in which my sacking was done,' Boon said. 'I was the only Tasmanian in the Australian team and they had shown no respect, let alone common courtesy to me.'

Stung to the very core, Boon stewed for a few days before receiving

an inquiring call from his Australian team-mate Dean Jones. Boon
and Pip flew to Melbourne soon after, where the meeting with
Redpath and Chambers took place. The Melbourne Cricket Club
and the Victorian Sheffield Shield team were the topics of
conversation – and more pertinently, Boon's admission to both.

And for all those Boon fans who feared the worst for all those
years during his development, rumours of jobs and Australian
selection from South Australia via the perfect wicket in Adelaide,
here is the crunch: 'They could have shoved a contract under my
nose and I would have signed it!' says Boon. But if Tasmania has
one man to thank for Boon staying in his home state, it is Ian
Redpath, the former Australian and Victorian right-hander.

'Ian "Redders" was just so logical. We just talked about cricket,
their plans and my ambitions,' Boon said. 'He talked about the
difference in real-estate values in Tasmania and Victoria, the
difficulties in uprooting my family, and employment opportunities
aside from cricket. He reminded me that I was the only Tasmanian
playing for Australia and, as such, had better opportunities in some
areas.'

'But Redders said that if I still decided that I wanted to come,
I would be made a member of the Sheffield Shield squad. It wasn't
like he was trying to recruit me; it was more like a father talking
to a son, discussing opportunities in business and life. I knew as
soon as I walked away from that meeting that I would stay in
Tasmania.'

3
ASHES AND
ISLANDS

ENGLAND 1985

David Boon was rated as a chance to make his first Ashes tour of England in 1981, when he was only 20 years old. However, Boon himself believed that his Sheffield Shield performances in the 1980–81 season hadn't been consistent enough.

'I thought I had more chance of making the World Cup team in 1983 after a good tour of Zimbabwe in the youth side and a reasonable Shield season. In 1981, rather than me thinking I'd go, it was more people telling me that I was a good chance to go. You start to hope, but being realistic, you should never expect it.

'By 1985, I had been picked for Australia the year before. But to be picked for any Ashes tour is the highlight of any Australian cricketer's career.' Boon was mindful that his friend Dean Jones, who had been picked for the 1984 tour of West Indies, missed out on England the next year.

On the day the '85 team was announced, Boon was shadowed by an ABC television crew from 9 am, awaiting the expected telephone call. However, the Australian touring party was announced on the radio news and the Board telephoned later.

'On the '85 tour I saw myself as being picked as the fifteenth, sixteenth or seventeenth. I was happy to be picked, but I thought that I would basically go and learn more about my cricket and play the county games. But in many ways I became like Greg Campbell in 1989, who by the way he performed in the preliminary games found himself in the first Test side.'

Boon actually played the first four Tests on the six-match tour – Headingley, Lord's, Trent Bridge and Old Trafford – and the one-day series. He was dropped for the last two Tests at Edgbaston and the Oval after seven Test innings, for a total of 124 runs, a highest score of 61 and an average of 17.71. In contrast, his overall tour figures of 838 runs at 55.86, including a high of 206 not out in twenty innings were more impressive.

England 1985, then, was certainly part of Boon's learning curve. Australia lost the tour 3–1, the direct opposite to the form of 1989, when Allan Border and his players romped home 4–0.

Before the '85 tour began, Australian cricket was rocked by the rumours surrounding the 'rebel' tours to South Africa. Crucially, four players had been picked for the Ashes tour whose names were alleged to be involved in the South African negotiations – Western Australian Graeme Wood, South Australian Wayne Phillips and New South Wales duo Dirk Wellham and Murray Bennett.

'We had all gathered in Melbourne and the South African business had broken,' Boon recalled. 'There were player meetings held whether the four of them should be allowed to tour – after they'd been picked! Simon O'Donnell and I were on our first tour and here we were being asked to vote on this issue. One by one, the players were brought into a room with the rest of the touring party, and Allan Border asked them questions about their involvement with the South African tour.'

Bans were imposed on the players who did go to South Africa – two seasons at first-class or Sheffield Shield level and three seasons in the national team. It was an emotional issue and time in Australian cricket: memories were still fresh of the split caused by World Series Cricket in the 1970s.

Australia began the 1985 tour as usual, with a one-day game against the Duchess of Norfolk's XI. However, because of numbers, Boon found himself playing in the opposition team on a freezing cold day at Arundel, where he made 34.

In the first Test at Headingley, Boon was trapped lbw by Graham Gooch for 14 in the first innings and bowled off his boot by Norman Cowans for 22 in the second. Australia was comprehensively beaten on a typical Headingley wicket. England made 533 as Australia bowled far too short, Tim Robinson top-scoring with 175 and Ian Botham making 60.

Despite this setback, the touring party went to Lord's full of confidence, because of Australia's excellent record at the home of cricket. There, Boon made four in the first innings, caught off the glove attempting to hook Botham. In the second innings, Boon was at the mercy of the man who was to become a personal bogey until 1988 – Phil Edmonds.

The English spinner was bowling around the wicket, concentrating on a rough patch outside Boon's leg-stump. 'There were bat-pads both sides of the wicket and in those days I wasn't being positive in my approach to spin bowling. Edmonds bowled and the ball hit the rough patch and bowled me middle and off. It must have turned a yard! I left the ground really upset.'

To make matters worse, at the next major interval, the Australian team was to be introduced to the Queen, Elizabeth II. 'I had just got out and we had to put on our blazers and go out onto the ground. I wasn't in any frame of mind to meet anyone. I've always wondered whether she thought I might have been rude, because all I could manage was a very quiet hello.'

In the third Test at Trent Bridge, England batted first and made 456. Australia led on the first innings after scoring 539, of which 15 runs were Boon's before he was caught and bowled by Emburey. England managed 2–196 in its second innings, rain causing a drawn result.

In the fourth Test at Old Trafford, Boon scored his only half-century in the second innings. He was twelfth man at Edgbaston in Birmingham and was omitted from the team for the sixth at the Oval.

'They say the first tour of England is the longest, but I couldn't get over how long it actually seemed. Or how hard it was to go out, day in and day out, to practice and play. Plus, obviously, we were losing.

'The 1989 tour, in comparison, was incredible because the shoe was on the other foot – Australia was winning the Test matches and England was getting flogged. We wanted to get out there, we wanted to practice. It was the classic example of the adage about when you're winning, everything goes well.'

Boon's life was made easier when Pip arrived for the second Test at Lord's and stayed on throughout.

When the tour ended, the Boons and Murray Bennett and his wife Jane went to Greece for a holiday, which meant that the Tasmanians returned home relaxed.

BOO-BOO

Dean Jones, the Australian and Victorian batsman, wrote this letter to David Boon after the Tasmanian was dropped from the fifth Test side to play England at the Sydney Cricket Ground in 1986–87.

'Boo-Boo

I'm just writing a little note to say that I know you'll be back! I felt very upset when I got dropped – the tears that came from my eyes will never be forgotten – especially now that I'm going okay!

I know what you are going through – not playing for Australia, not being with your mates – very heart-breaking. But I know you too well to sit back, and you will come back a better player – I know I did!

I will never forget our time we had in Jaipur, which I felt 'bridged' the gap for me from a first-class player to a Test player. You gave me confidence in your own little way, which no one has done before. I will never forget that.

I am not writing to help stop the pain in your guts – just trying to get your thoughts into perspective. You are the *second best batter* in the country outside AB, and we (and I) need you.

Never feel sorry for yourself or get pissed off with the game because it will get worse, time and time again.

Again I know how you're feeling. But I want to bat and be with you again, because it was enjoyable – I don't like being away from my mates. But more importantly, not only am I proud that you are my mate, but I am proud in the way you have handled success and the kicks in the guts.

That's why you are someone very special to me.

See you soon.

Deano.

PS Just a thought – have a look at your old video clips and see what you were doing right then compared to now.

Love to Pip.'

ENGLAND 1989

David Boon's second tour of England was preceded by an honour of a different sort: he was named a Member of the British Empire. 'It was a bit of shock, getting recognised like that – I was only twenty-eight – it was a huge honour,' Boon said.

And Boon admitted to a minor subterfuge in an attempt to be invested with the gong by Queen Elizabeth. 'At the first investiture, I couldn't attend because of work. Then someone had the idea that if I was going to England on tour, I might be able to be included in a ceremony conducted by the Queen herself.'

However, the Governor of Tasmania, Sir Phillip Bennett, was far too sharp for Boon when the second investiture was announced.

'The Governor's aide-de-camp rang me and said, "Sir Phillip has checked with your boss. You have no work commitments this time and he wants to present the MBE to you!" I don't think I've ever worn it, apart from that day. And I don't sign my name "MBE".'

For Boon and his Australian team-mates, the tour of England in 1989 was almost the exact opposite of 1985. In '85, Australia won the one-day Texaco series and lost the Test series 3–1; in '89, England won the one-dayers and Australia triumphed in the Test arena 4–0.

The Australian squad of seventeen was also different for at least one reason – Boon was joined by his Tasmanian Sheffield Shield team-mate Greg Campbell. 'For the first time there was another Tasmanian in the squad and everyone was pleasantly surprised by the way he went,' Boon said. He bowled so well in the preliminary games that he forced his way into the first Test side. And he got a wicket, Derek Pringle, leg before wicket.

'I remember having a chat with him afterwards and telling him, "If you never play again, no one can take that wicket away from you – you've got a Test wicket."'

At the opening match, against the Duchess of Norfolk's XI at Arundel, Boon scored 114 not out, retiring 'hurt'. That was also the match which made headlines when Allan Border slogged a six, the ball breaking the nose of a woman watching the game from a deckchair.

Boon went to England perhaps more single-minded than ever before, which is a major statement for a man who is extremely intense about his cricket. He was also one of the fittest Australians in pre-tour calculations and was even rated as the one with least body fat.

His first tour of England still haunted him, despite conquering the bogey of John Emburey's spin in Australia during the 1988 Bicentennial Test match with 184 not out. 'In England in '85, I scored county runs but none in the Tests. I wanted to show the English people that I could play a lot better than that. Obviously, there were four years' difference in my cricket, but I still hadn't been successful in England, one of the benchmarks of an Australian player.'

Australia played the MCC at Lord's in a one-day match, and Geoff Marsh and Boon broke an Australian record, scoring 277 from 300 balls. Australia made 309 and Boon contributed 166, in one over hitting Vic Marks for five fours and two sixes. 'One of the fours was a reverse sweep. Thankfully, Simmo was out in the back of the rooms and didn't see it,' Boon said.

Against Somerset at Taunton, Boon made 61 in the first innings; against Middlesex, he made 20 and 86 at Lord's. Boon scored 172 from 157 balls in a one-day match, in which Dean Jones made 89, at Headingley against Yorkshire.

In the first Texaco Trophy match at Old Trafford, England made 231 to Australia's 136, Boon scored five. In the second one-dayer, England made 5–226, Allan Lamb the major scorer with 100 not out; Australia made 8–226. The game wasn't declared a tie; instead, it was decided to leave the game in limbo until the third and final match. 'It was decided that unless the series was drawn, the match would be regarded as a tie. But if series was drawn, then the side that had lost the least wickets – England – would win,' Boon said.

'I believe the rule should have applied in the first place.'

Australia won the third Texaco match at Lord's, scoring 4-279, Marsh made 111 not out, to England's 7–278, in which captain Graham Gooch made 100. 'England was named series winner because of the confusing business in the second game, losing less wickets than we did.'

He missed the next match against Warwickshire at Edgbaston because of a chest infection, which needed antibiotic treatment.

Boon returned against Derbyshire and made 34 on an ordinary wicket, but suffered an injured left hand when he was struck by medium-pacer Simon Base. 'It hit the bottom of my left hand and it blew up when I took my glove off. The x-ray showed a bent bone, but no break. I can still feel the depression in my hand,' Boon said. 'But it came good before the first Test.'

Australia went to Headingley for what was to be the start of the Mark Taylor–Steve Waugh show. 'We had bowled too short at Headingley in '85, but traditionally, if you win the toss, everyone bowls at Headingley. AB won the toss and we batted, the plan being to give ourselves an edge to start with – I think England were taken aback by the tactic.'

Boon made only nine, caught behind by Jack Russell from a Neil Foster leg-cutter. But Australia amassed 7-601 declared. Taylor made 136 and Waugh 150 not out, both Test debuts in England; Border made 66 and Jones 79.

England made 430, Lamb scoring 100, Kim Barnett 80 and Robin Smith 60.

Boon made 43 in the second innings before he was adjudged lbw to Phillip de Freitas by umpire John Holder. 'After he gave me out, I kept staring at him. But I have a lot of respect for John Holder, because he called me into the umpires' room after the day's play,' Boon said. 'He was really upset and apologised to me for making a terrible decision. Whether you believe umpires should or shouldn't talk to players about a certain decision, it still took a lot of guts for him to admit to me that he had made a bad one.'

Australia declared its second innings closed at 3–230 and bowled England out for 191 in 55 overs to win the match by 210 runs. Terry Alderman took 5–44 to add to his 5–107 in the first innings. The Australians were understandably ecstatic, celebrating their country's first-ever victory at Leeds.

However, the hectic tour schedule meant that the Australian team travelled to Manchester that night by bus to play Lancashire the next day. To say that the traditional post-victory ales had an affect on the players might be over-stating the situation, but more than one Australian was 'a tad weary' in Boon-speak.

Allan Border had the game off, so too did Alderman, leading to his now-legendary nickname of 'Test-match Terry', because of the negligible number of tour games in which the Western Australian played.

Australia, with Geoff Marsh as acting-captain won the toss and decided to bowl first. Boon was fielding at bat-pad as usual, but was wearing full rubber-soled shoes as opposed to the regular half-spikes. Greg Campbell, who went on to be Man of the Match, was bowling, when Boon stopped a very crisp shot played off Lancashire batsman Nick Speak's pads. Boon stood up and gestured to his team-mates, indicating that tired or not, he was on his mettle. A couple of deliveries later, Campbell bounced Speak and the fun began. The English right-hander fended at the ball and it came off his glove and ballooned upwards in Boon's direction. 'I looked up at the ball, tried to take one step and fell over face-first. I didn't even touch the ball, which landed in front of my nose. Everyone on the field, except perhaps for Greg, was laughing. Swamp was standing at first slip with tears in his eyes he was laughing so hard. In the next three overs we dropped about five catches. Speak made 26 and was dropped four times!'

Lancashire made 184, to which Australia replied with 288, Boon dismissed for a duck, caught down leg-side off the bowling of former Tasmanian import and West Indian paceman Patrick Patterson. Australia ended up winning the game by nine wickets,

Boon making 23 not out in the second innings.

Australia then beat Northamptonshire easily before heading to Lord's for the second Test.

England batted first and made 286. Australia, wavering at 6–276, went on to post a total of 528, in which Steve Waugh made 152 not out. In partnership with Waugh, the tail not only wagged but contributed considerably: paceman Geoff Lawson made 74, Merv Hughes 36 and Trevor Hohns 24.

Boon made 94. In truth, this remains one of his greatest disappointments – to come so close to a century at Lord's. 'The biggest thing I remember is getting out on 94. To score a hundred at Lord's would mean a lot to any cricketer, being the home of cricket. I had been concentrating on playing straight and Graham Dilley bowled me an out-swinger. Graham Gooch was the one slip, there was a third man and ring field. I tried to run the ball to third man, but nicked it off the face of the bat to Graham. Of course, you'd rather score 94 than nothing in any match. But inwardly I was really peeved, because a hundred at Lord's would have meant so much to me.'

Boon soon made amends for his personal disappointment in the second innings by once again saving his country from a perilous situation. England made 359 in its second innings, Gooch scoring 100 and Robin Smith 59, which left Australia 119 to win. Not a major task, but as so often happens in the game of cricket, England was able to break through – Marsh one, Taylor 27, Border one and Jones a duck. That left Australia at 4–67. Boon and Steve Waugh saw Australia through to victory, the Tasmanian scoring 58 not out and the New South Welshman undefeated on 21.

Boon's parents, Clarrie and Lesley, rate that innings as one their son's finest ever. Few people disagree, although the number of times Boon's bat has directed or saved his country continues to grow.

As the Australian players watched nervously from the balcony, Border found himself involved in one of the tour's now-legendary superstitions. After Border had been dismissed, he had left the viewing area to have a shower and shave. Whenever he tried to return to the balcony, his players would send him back indoors. 'He was in the bathroom all afternoon,' Boon laughed. 'He must have showered five times and shaved three times because the boys wouldn't let him back in.'

Apparently, Border had also made mention of the fatal Test at Headingley in 1981, when Australia required only 130 to win on the last day and were bowled over for 111. Cricketers being superstitious animals, Border was first abused and then banished to the bathroom.

Although Australia was 2–0 up and Steve Waugh after three innings in two Tests had scored 350 undismissed runs – and subsequently had no average – from Border down the players kept stressing and repeating that this was a six-Test tour, not five and that at some stage during it, Australia would struggle.

Of course, the England selectors added to the unfolding drama of Australia's impending whitewash by recalling Ian Botham for the third Test at Edgbaston. 'In the first two Tests, as a team we had been able to exert more pressure on England than vice versa. But we went into the third Test determined to treat the situation as though it were 0–0, rather than the reality of 2–0.'

Australia batted first on day one at Birmingham and was 4–232 at stumps. Boon was batting with Dean Jones who hammered Paul Jarvis back down the wicket. Jarvis dived, got a touch to the ball before it continued on to dislodge the bails, running out Boon at the non-striker's end for 38. It was his first experience of being 'tipped' out.

Of course, Botham got into the act with the very first ball of the innings, hitting Mark Taylor on the pads and going into a huge appeal – even though it wasn't even close.

'The wicket did a bit, but the England bowlers, except for Botham, all bowled too short,' Boon said. 'Jones was 71 not out, Tubbsy (Taylor) got 42 and Swamp 42, but the Fleet Street papers were full of Botham. The hype was on and to a certain extent, there was life back in the series again because of Beefy's return.'

To this time on tour, the Australians had enjoyed superb weather in England, but this state of affairs didn't last. The Edgbaston Test ended in a draw as the heavens over Birmingham opened and the ground was flooded. Actually, Edgbaston possesses perhaps the only 'full-ground' covers in international cricket. But at the back of the dressing room, the water was a foot deep.

Steve Waugh was dismissed for the first time in three Tests, which won all the headlines, while Jones's century was largely ignored.

The Australian touring party adjourned to Scotland after the Edgbaston Test for a day hosted by the tour sponsors at Fintry Castle, outside of Glasgow. The day was spent in a semi-serious Highland Games, as the Australian players tried their hands at haggis-throwing and tug-o-war. Wisely, they weren't allowed to attempt tossing the caber.

Boon, Tom Moody and Carl Rackemann decided to join the festivities whole-heartedly by wearing kilts. Boon in Ray-Ban sunglasses and a kilt is an interesting mental image, but better photograph!

'In the haggis-throwing competition, we had to stand on a special barrel, complete the throw and not fall off,' Boon said. 'Big Tom threw his haggis 236 feet – we were using imperial measurements because we were in the Mother Country. That broke a 70-year-old record of 186 feet.'

For Boon, another memorable Scottish experience was playing golf at the Royal and Ancient Club of St Andrews. 'Playing golf at St Andrews is like playing cricket at Lord's – it's the home of the game. It was totally different to Australian and American golf courses, being a traditional links course: it's eight holes out, straight into the wind, two across and eight home with the wind at your back. Playing into the wind, you'd hit a driver and a three-wood on a par four and not even get close. Or with the wind behind, you'd hit the ball perfectly, walk up the fairway and find it deep in a four-by-four bunker!'

The Australians played some of the great British courses – St Andrews, The Belfry, and Sunningdale. 'Watching different tournaments on television, you can see the holes you've played,' Boon says now. 'At The Belfry I was 80 metres behind Seve Ballesteros' longest drive, which is marked by a special plaque beside the fairway.'

In Scotland, Australia also played a one-day match. Boon bowled and took two wickets, much to the delight of a improbable, but extremely vocal, pro-Tasmanian crowd. After play closed, Boon adjourned to the outer for an ale or two with his new-found fans.

Back in England, the next tour game was against Hampshire – where Boon had scored a galling pair in 1985. 'A few people made mention of that fact, including Hampshire captain Mark Nicholas, when I first went out to bat,' Boon said. He and Steve Waugh each made centuries, ending that memory.

The next game was against Gloucestershire, which was rivalled – for both home country and Australian touring party interest – by the coinciding British Open golf. Boon made 16 in a first innings total of 4–438 declared; Mark Taylor made 141 and Jones 123.

'That was the year that Mark Calvecchio won the British Open after a three-way play-off,' Boon said. 'To be honest, there was probably more interest in the golf for us. Tim Zoehrer won heaps, because he backed Calvecchio early.

'We bowled Gloucester out for 92 in under two hours and Geoff Lawson took 6–30. But the most memorable thing about that game was the messages that kept coming out from the dressing room about the golf. As soon as it was over, we all tore off the ground to watch the last few holes.'

Geoff Lawson's form continued in the fourth Test at Old Trafford. The former New South Wales skipper, who retired from first-class cricket at the end of the 1991–92 domestic season, took 6–72 as England was bowled out for 260; Robin Smith made 143. Australia replied with 441, of which Boon made 12 – dismissed by an Angus

Fraser delivery which he let go by, only to hear it knock back his off-stump.

England's second innings began disastrously: 6–120 at tea on the fourth day. But Jack Russell's 126 not out and John Emburey's 64 at least got England to 264. Which left Australia 81 runs to win the Ashes on English soil – the prize which had eluded the tourists since 1948, when Don Bradman's team succeeded. Geoff Marsh and Mark Taylor were cruising toward victory when Boon made a magnanimous, but expected gesture, to his captain Border.

'I said to AB, "If we only need a few, you deserve to be out there and I'll gladly step aside."'

'No, you deserve it as much as I do,' was Border's reply.

Marsh was dismissed and Boon went out to join Taylor. Boon made 10 not out, the final four of which produced the winning runs. 'It wasn't the most classical sweep shot, but Nick Cook bowled on the spot and the fielders were up,' Boon said. 'I didn't have it in mind to hit the winning runs, but the ball went for four. I'll never forget that moment.'

However, after the initial ecstasy, there was also a sombre note. 'AB spent a lot of time with David Gower, who was understandably dejected by the magnitude of the defeat, 3–0 after four Tests,' Boon said. 'And Border wasn't just simply saying, "I know how you feel", because he knew. We were beaten 3–1 by England in 1985. I don't reckon we sang our victory song until an hour or more after the match, because AB was tied up talking to Gower and the media.'

In the annals of cricket, the two tours of 1985 and '89 will be forever overshadowed by the spectre of apartheid. Before the '85 tour, Australian cricket was torn apart by the announcement of the rebel tours of South Africa. At Old Trafford in '89, the news of England's own rebel touring party was announced, severely debilitating the English squad.

Despite the wait, the Australians did manage to celebrate in gargantuan proportions. However, the tour schedule required the Australians to play Nottinghamshire at Trent Bridge the next morning.

The bus duly arrived at the Notts ground and acting-captain Marsh walked out to conduct the tossing of the coin. Marsh lost. The Notts captain was of the opinion that he and his team should bat. Marsh differed.

'But I won the toss, I get to choose,' was the county team skipper's thoroughly logical argument.

'You may have won the toss but I've got no bowlers – they're all asleep – you couldn't bat if you wanted to!' Marsh replied. The Nottingham captain deferred and Australia batted.

During that week, Boon found himself in the wars fielding at bat-pad. On the first occasion, in the county game, Derek Randall struck Boon in the helmet from a Carl Rackemann delivery. In the fifth Test, Boon received a thunderous blow – resulting in a depressed fracture of the cheekbone – to the head by Robin Smith off Trevor Hohns's bowling.

'The helmet just disintegrated. Deano found a piece of perspex from the helmet 110 paces from where I was fielding,' Boon said. 'I went off for a lie down, and luckily the next day was a rest day in the Test match. It was a bad week at bat-pad, really.'

The Trent Bridge Test was where Mark Taylor and Geoff Marsh decided to create even more mental strain for Boon – by batting the entire first day of the match. 'It was the hardest day I've ever had, six hours with the pads on. You just sit there, concentrating on every ball and the waiting just gets harder and harder.'

The opening pair made 300 in the day and had a partnership of 329, Marsh out with 20 minutes still to play before the lunch interval on the following day. 'All the lads had started to rib me – "Everyone knows what happens after a big partnership! More than one bloke gets out!"' Boon said. 'And at lunch I was still nought not out!'

Boon went on to make 73 before he was stumped. Australia made 6–602 declared. Marsh made 137, Taylor 219 and Border 65. Incredibly, Steve Waugh made a duck – giving Devon Malcolm his first Test wicket. Waugh hit the ball like a rocket, but it went straight to David Gower at backward square leg.

England was 5–130 at stumps on the third day and Smith was unbeaten on 78, having already despatched Boon to the pavilion with his head injury. England went on to scrape together 246, then followed on and was dismissed for 167 in its second innings. A victory by an innings and 180-odd runs on probably the best wicket the Australians played on during the tour, was their easiest win.

The next game, against Kent, again demonstrated the gambling prowess of reserve wicketkeeper Tim Zoehrer. Australia declared at 8–356, its overnight total, of which Boon made 86 and Jones 128. The match was drawn, Kent making 191 and 237. But this was the instance in which Australian off-spinner Tim May hit his first six on any oval in any form of cricket. Jones lost five hundred very large English pounds to Zoehrer!

In the final Test match at the Oval, Graham Gooch returned to the English team, having stepped aside of his own volition at Trent Bridge. The Australians were perplexed by Gooch's decision.

'We had definitely worked him out through the mid-wicket region. But were disappointed, because he was, and is, a very good mate of AB's,' Boon said. 'In 1986, when I had a bad trot, I knew the axe was coming, but I would never have pulled out. However, Gooch did have injuries and other pressures.' His return was short-lived – lbw to Terry Alderman for a duck.

Australia made 468 to complete its astonishing record of 400-plus Test innings. Jones scored 122, Mark Taylor 71 and Border 76; Boon made 46. England avoided the follow-on via captain Gower's 79 in a total of 285. Australia declared its second innings closed at 4–219: Mark Taylor 48, Boon 37 run out, Border 51 and Jones 50. On the last day England was 5–143, with Smith on 77, when bad light stopped play after intermittent rain. The 1989 tour of England was complete.

The statistics for the Test series are extremely revealing. England used 28 players for the six matches; Australia fielded only 13 of its 17 tourists. Robin Smith played five Tests and scored 553 runs at an average of 61.44. Jack Russell made 314 runs at 39.25 in six matches. The next recognised batsman was the England skipper, Gower, with an average of 34.81. Without those three players, how might England have fared?

In contrast, five of Australia's first six batsmen posted Test averages of 50-plus. Steve Waugh headed the list with 506 runs at the superlative rate of 126.50. Mark Taylor was next with 839 runs, the leading aggregate scorer, at 83.9. Allan Border was third with 442 at 73.66; Dean Jones had 566 at 70.75 and Boon himself contributed 442 at 55.25.

The bowling figures complemented the batting. Australia fielded only six bowlers through the Tests; England used 15. Terry Alderman was the destroyer with 41 wickets at an average of only 17.36 runs. Trevor Hohns took 11 wickets at 27.27, the identical average to Geoff Lawson, who was second in total with 29 victims. Merv Hughes had an average of 32.36 and dismissed 19 batsmen.

In comparison, Neil Foster was England's most successful bowler with 12 wickets at 35.08 even though he played only three Tests before joining the rebel tour to South Africa. Angus Fraser was next in line with nine at 35.88.

WEST INDIES 1991

Australia's tour of the West Indies in 1991 was billed as 'The World Championship of Cricket'. Media hype? Certainly. But after the crushing 4–0 Ashes tour of England in 1989, the rejuvenated Australia squad hadn't played the West Indies in a Test series – although the Caribbean cricketers had been to Australia the season before for a one-day series. Australia retained the Ashes in 1990-91 at home, the perfect build-up for the tour to the West Indies.

Although still led by captain Vivian Richards, with his ageing but still superlative batting pair Gordon Greenidge and Desmond Haynes, the Australian cricket press, and many of the players themselves thought that the great West Indian combination might at last be vulnerable.

Boon himself had scored 530 runs at 75.21 during the preceding summer, which included a Test century of 121 at the Adelaide Oval. But the West Indies was a different experience for Boon, on his first tour to this group of islands which stretches west from Cuba, south of Florida to the coast of Venezuela, above which lies Trinidad.

The Australian touring party's first game was on St Kitts, against a President's XI. The team stayed in a hotel on the beach in bungalows, Boon rooming with left-arm paceman Bruce Reid, who unfortunately was again to suffer a Test series interrupted by injury, and wicketkeeper Ian Healy, who became involved in the tour's major controversy.

On the second day of the game against St Kitts, the Australians were to discover the West Indian approach to dealing with a perennial cricket problem. 'There was a huge tropical storm, the rain pelting down, and the covers just weren't adequate enough to stop the water,' Boon said. 'When the storm ended, only the areas around the batting creases were affected, not the actual wicket itself. But rather than use sawdust to soak up the water or a 'Super-Sopper' as we do in Australia, the curator came out, poured petrol over the affected areas and lit it! He literally burnt the moisture out of the ground. It certainly worked, but the surface became very brittle.' The game was drawn, but Mark Taylor started his tour with a century, 101, in the second innings.

Onto Jamaica, where Australia was to play the first Test. There the wicket was relatively new, but the Australians were pleased to play on it, despite it being somewhat up and down, because they discovered it took spin.

Boon said that throughout the tour, because West Indian practice facilities – the nets at various first-class and Test grounds – weren't up to international standard, centre wicket sessions became paramount.

The tour game in Jamaica was where Craig McDermott was struck in the face by a delivery from West Indian paceman Courtney Walsh. In hindsight, this became a major omen for the tail-end of Australia's batting. And McDermott's batting continued to suffer as a result of this injury.

In the opening one-day international, Australia scored 4–244 and defeated the West Indies, which made 209. Boon hit 34, Dean Jones 88 not out and Mark Waugh 67; Craig McDermott took 4–34 from 8.5 overs.

Jamaica is also the home of Michael Holding, the former Tasmanian Sheffield Shield import, who is a great friend of Boon's.

'The capital of Jamaica, Kingston, is a scary place,' Boon said. 'To get to the ground, we had to go past the Kingston jail, which supposedly has one of the biggest death rows in the world on a per capita basis. Every morning on our way to practice, the inmates would hang out through the bars and shout out what the West Indies were going to do to us. They kept yelling, "Licks! Licks!" and cracking their fingers, which was their version of us getting hit with a cricket ball.

'But that attitude was everywhere, but not usually in an aggressive manner. The West Indies have been on top for so long, their supporters rib you because they think they're going to beat you.'

Because Jamaica, particularly Kingston, has such a reputation for violence and disorder, the Australian players were warned not to venture out alone. 'In 14 days, I didn't go out on my own,' Boon said with a laugh. 'I probably only went out twice, once to go with Michael Holding to his favourite Chinese restaurant and another time for a few beers at an English tavern.'

Cricket throughout the West Indies is a way of life, and people play the game in the streets and on the beaches. However, Boon noted that the West Indian officials are worried about the depth of young talent in their game, because of the inroads that professional basketball is making.

For several years now, the West Indies have received American cable television, which brings the athleticism and skills of the US

National Basketball Association into their living rooms. 'The officials are very concerned that cricket may be losing its influence,' Boon said.

As an overview, Boon said that the West Indies – which remain reassuringly cricket-mad – differ to the sub-continent. 'Indian fans are more fanatical. They know everything about you and all about cricket's rules,' Boon said. 'They recall innings you've played five or six years ago, the shots you played and even your stats. In the West Indies, it's more like a big party. In the Test in Antigua and Barbados, there was music and dancing all day, 20,000 people enjoying a party with cricket in the middle of the ground.

'There was only ever a hint of real aggression from the crowds during the tour. In Jamaica, the spectators just wanted someone – anyone – to get hit by a bouncer. When Gus Logie got hit in Jamaica, you could almost sense the crowd's approval. Maybe we were getting the wrong impression of the collective feeling. But they seemed to have an immense appreciation of bouncers – no matter who bowled them.'

The first Test in Jamaica was drawn, after one and a half days were lost to rain. West Indies scored 264 in the first innings, Gus Logie making 77 not out; McDermott took 5–80 and Merv Hughes 4–67. Boon scored 109 not out, his tenth Test century, in Australia's first innings of 371. Geoff Marsh made 69 and Mark Taylor 58. West Indies made 3–334 in their second innings, Richie Richardson unbeaten on 104.

It was also in Jamaica that another chapter in Boon's now-legendary personal book of 'pain management' was written. He was struck a thudding blow on the chin by Patrick Patterson, the former Tasmanian Sheffield Shield import. Rather than come in for treatment, Boon was patched up by Australian physiotherapist Errol Alcott beside the pitch. After the innings closed, Boon received a necessary stitch – forgoing any anaesthetic – from a West Indian doctor, who excitedly told the crowd, milling outside the dressing room, of the Australian's courage!

Boon said that the Australians had been pleased with the aggressive manner in which they had performed in Jamaica.

In the second one-day game in Port of Spain, Trinidad, Australia took a 2–0 lead in the series after making 172 and dismissing West Indies for 127; McDermott and Mike Whitney each took three wickets.

The third limited-overs contest was also played in Trinidad, with the West Indies achieving what was to be their solitary win in a rain-affected contest.

The fourth one-dayer saw Australia win the series 3–1. Australia made 6–283; Marsh scored 113, Border 79 and Mark Waugh 49. West Indies were all out 246; Mark Waugh took 3–34, McDermott, Steve Waugh and Bruce Reid two wickets each.

Boon missed the fourth 50-over game in Bridgetown, Barbados, after being struck on the left foot by a Mark Waugh delivery during practice. 'I was wearing rubbers in the nets and Mark hit me with a yorker on my big toe,' Boon said. 'I had an x-ray, but they couldn't find a crack. But the next day, I couldn't walk! It was aching all the time for the rest of the tour. When I got home, I had another x-ray and they discovered there'd been a crack there all along.'

The last one-day international was played at the Bourda Ground in Georgetown, Guyana. West Indies made 251, but was overhauled by Australia with fifteen balls to spare. Marsh made 106 and Border 60.

In the second Test in Guyana, however, Boon said that, in retrospect, the players reverted to a lesser mental state – survival, as opposed to playing positive, attacking cricket. 'We were looking to bat for time, which is the wrong tack to take against West Indies. If you don't get runs, they're eventually going to get something through you. The West Indies have got a very good bowling attack and even when faced with a flat wicket, they just revert to line and length, content to frustrate you out.'

Australia made 348 in its first innings, Boon scoring nine before being given out in controversial circumstances. Boon was struck on the top of the pad, clearly outside the line of the stumps, by

Malcolm Marshall, the ball continuing through on the up to wicketkeeper Jeff Dujon. The West Indians appealed simultaneously for lbw and caught behind. Umpire Clyde Duncan, standing in his maiden Test, gave the decision, and informed the official scorers – one had inscribed lbw, the other caught behind – that the latter had been the form of dismissal.

It was in Guyana that Richie Richardson, Viv Richards' heir apparent, made 182 of a total of 569, as the Australian bowlers served up half-volley after half-volley to him. Richardson was particularly severe on Merv Hughes.

'The quicker Merv tried to bowl them, the quicker they hit the fence,' Boon said. 'We had posted a gully very square, a third man and a deep point. But Guyana is a very quick ground – five metres either side of a fieldsman and you just couldn't cut the ball off. Richardson hit the ball consistently all day, a great knock.'

It was in Australia's second innings that the huge controversy surrounding Dean Jones's dismissal arose. 'Jones was bowled by a no-ball and he walked away to cover, not having heard the no-ball call because of the huge noise that erupted from the crowd after his wicket was broken,' Boon said. 'Carl Hooper ran over with the ball and pulled the stump out of the ground and the run-out was given out.'

In the press box and commentary positions around the ground, journalists consulted their *Wisdens*. The consensus was that umpire Clyde Cumberbatch had made the wrong decision. He later admitted his error. Jones should have been recalled to the wicket because a batsman cannot be run out unless he is attempting a run – and Jones clearly was leaving the wicket under the belief that he had been dismissed.

This incident merely increased the level of ill-feeling between the teams that had arisen since the breakdown of the 'socialisation' policy. Australian captain Allan Border was extremely angry about Umpire Cumberbatch's decision.

Australia was all out 248 in its second innings; the West Indies made 0–31 to record a 10-wicket victory and take a 1–0 lead in the series.

Despite the defeat, Boon and his team-mates found time for a practical joke at the expense of friend and West Indian wicketkeeper Jeff Dujon. 'There were a lot of kids at the ground. Some of them had killed a poisonous snake in the moat around the ground,' Boon said, 'so we nabbed it from them and placed it just where Dujon would stand when he came out to 'keep. He came out and saw the snake lying in the grass and visibly jumped. Then he just turned and stared at the Australian dressing room . . .'

Boon was struck by the dilapidated state of Guyana, a country where inflation had sent the currency skyrocketing. 'It was costing us $700 Guyanan for an ordinary meal,' Boon said. 'We had a team dinner and it cost $15,000! You had to carry an enormous wad of money in your wallet.

'But you see all these magnificent old buildings from colonial days, which haven't been touched by a paintbrush for twenty years. The grandeur of the place remains, but it's a very poor country.'

The next tour game was against the West Indies Under-23s at Kingston, St Vincent. The young Caribbeans made 307 and Australia replied with 390; Mark Taylor made 122, Boon 53, Jones 60 and Steve Waugh 85. Peter Taylor took 5–37 with his off-spin in the Under-23s' second innings of 9–162, a narrow escape from defeat.

The third Test was at Port of Spain in Trinidad, which finished in a draw because of bad weather. 'For two days we went down to the ground, watched the clouds and rain coming over the mountains, and then went back to the hotel,' Boon said.

Australia managed 1–55 from 23 overs on the first day and 294 for the first innings; West Indies made 227 in reply and Australia declared its second innings closed at 3–123. Boon was struck on the middle joint of his left index finger in the first innings, again by Patrick Patterson.

The Barbados Test was the one which first tantalised Australia with the hint of victory and then dashed it in the team's face. Australia bowled first and dismissed the West Indies for 149. McDermott took 4–94, Hughes 4–44 and Reid, who had rejoined the team after back problems, the other two wickets. The opportunity to level the series was upon the tourists. But for the last ten years, the West Indies' strength has been such that whenever the batsmen miss out, the bowlers make amends. They bowled Australia out for 134. Courtney Walsh took 4–14 and Marshall 3–60 in the rout.

West Indies declared its second innings at 9–536, leaving the Australians 552 for victory, or more crucially, a day and a half to bat through to save the match. 'Australia was all out for 208 in the second innings. Swamp was given out first ball to what was a questionable lbw,' Boon said. 'Mark Taylor made 76, I got 57 and Jones made 37. But the game was over by tea-time. After Barbados, the so-called battle for the world championship of cricket was over.' Ambrose and Marshall each took three wickets and Walsh and Carl Hooper two each to seal the Test match series.

The fifth and final Test was held in Antigua, where former West Indian pace legend Andy Roberts was curator. In keeping with Roberts' playing days, the wicket was quick and bouncy, the only one of its type the Australians saw on tour.

'The wicket should have suited the West Indies, but Australia played consistently, where we hadn't in the Test matches before,' Boon said. 'Mark Waugh made a 100 in the first innings. The West Indians had felt that Mark had a weakness playing against pure pace bowling and had been after him from day one of the tour. It was a hundred that took a lot of guts, because he took a lot of balls on the hands early.'

Australia made 403, dismissing West Indies for 214. Mark Taylor made 144 in Australia's second innings of 265, Boon the next highest scorer with 35. The West Indies were bowled out for 297, a loss by 157 runs. Hughes took two wickets, but Australia's fielding did the damage with three run outs.

'We beat the West Indies in four days. It was good to get on the scoreboard and finish the tour on a winning note. We went down 2–1 rather than 2–0 or 3–0.

Boon described the tour as one of the most difficult he has experienced, because of the problems the Australians encountered travelling from one island to the next. 'We would often spend two weeks in one spot, except for interludes for tour games on the smaller islands,' Boon said.

He appreciated Barbados, where the touring party stayed in self-contained apartments. Boon, Marsh and Reid would get together for self-cooked feasts. 'We even invited AB to a home-cooked meal one night,' Boon said. 'I was chef and Swamp and Reidy were chief bottle-washers. I cooked chicken, steak and vegetables and prepared salads. It's fair to say AB enjoyed my cooking!'

On the island of St Vincent, where Australia had played the West Indian Under-23s, Boon and Marsh ended up on a 'Cook's Tour' of the tiny volcanic outcrop. 'After the game we went to a function at the local bank manager's house. It was a barbeque and Swamp and I started talking to a local,' Boon said. 'The team bus was going, but this guy said, "I'll look after you," so we stayed. At about 10 o'clock, he said that he'd give us a lift home and we got the guided tour of St Vincent.

'We saw the local church, the old fort and the library. He drove past the Australia team hotel and kept going – to a pub called the Lime and Green for a nightcap. We got home about one o'clock in the morning – it was a three-hour ride home!'

At the tour's close, the Australian party returned home to Australia via Bermuda, at the invitation of the local cricket community and Robert Stigwood, the famous film producer. 'Bermuda is a little like an English village,' Boon said. 'We all hired mopeds and immediately called ourselves the Hells Angels, powering around everywhere at the speed limit of 20 kph.'

4
HOME AND
AWAY 1992–93

HOME: VERSUS THE WEST INDIES

For the first Test match against the West Indies at the 'Gabba in December 1992, David Boon found himself returning to a role he had relinquished on the Ashes tour of England in 1989 – that of Australia's opening batsman.

After successfully partnering Geoff Marsh, with whom he started so many Australian innings at Test and one-day level, Boon was 'promoted' up the order from number three, the position to which he is best-suited, to join left-hander Mark Taylor.

Marsh had been dropped for the last Test in Perth against India in 1991–92, replaced by Victorian Wayne Phillips, who lasted only one match. Western Australian Tom Moody partnered Taylor on the three-Test tour of Sri Lanka.

'There had been some media talk about me opening again, but

in the Australian XI game against West Indies in Hobart, Matthew
Hayden and Wayne Phillips opened and I batted at three,' recalls
Boon.

Australian coach Bob Simpson and fellow national selector John
Benaud were also at the Australian XI game and expressed interest
in the Tasmanian Sheffield Shield side which was announced to
play against South Australia in Adelaide.

'They said, "You're not opening in Adelaide, are you?" I told them
that Dene Hills and Nick Courtney would be, and they said, "Good,
good". But when the Test side was picked a few days later I realised
I'd be back opening because there no-one else in the team!

'Both Simmo and Allan Border explained the situation to me in
Brisbane. They thought the West Indies' pace attack would be better
countered by taking a positive approach into the games – picking
stroke-makers through the middle order – Steve Waugh, Mark
Waugh, Dean Jones and Damien Martyn.'

Boon agreed to the move.

However, five months later, on the eve of the 1993 Ashes tour
of England, Boon was again released from the opening responsibility
and allowed back to his preferred number-three position.

'I suppose in a way I do, deep down, have a personal preference
for three. But I opened with Swampy and did another summer with
Tubby (Taylor) – it doesn't bother me. I bat where the team needs
me.'

The positive approach was stressed three days before the series
against the West Indies began, with the Australian team holding
a meeting at the Brisbane Dockside Parkroyal. There is nothing
new in the Australians having a team meeting, but this time it was
brought forward from the traditional match eve gathering.

'It was a different approach. The theory, that of Allan Border and
Bob Simpson, was to have our game plan in our minds throughout
our final training. The plan was that everybody would be positive,
more so the batting. Positive in that we would bat within our own
limitations and strengths.

'Because the West Indies are masters of getting you into a situation of just trying to survive – and with a four-pronged pace attack, that's never going to work. So if you were a strong cutter of the ball, you were to play that strength.'

Australia won the toss and batted on the first morning at the 'Gabba. Victorian right-hander and team stalwart Dean Jones was relegated to twelfth-man. Western Australian Damien Martyn made his Test debut. Jones had been restricted to only three single opportunities to score runs because of bad weather, while Martyn had reeled off consecutive hundreds in the Shield game against Queensland.

'The first day of a Test series is really important – it can set the trend for a whole series. Plus, we knew that the West Indies had absolutely whupped us in the last two or three matches at the 'Gabba, so we really tried to get stuck in on that first day,' Boon said.

'As a batter, I hadn't faced Ian Bishop for a long time. He had evolved in a similar fashion to Malcolm Marshall, having come on his first series as the fifth, one-day bowler. But on this tour Bishop was regarded as one of the quickest in the world and reputedly one of the best.

'From the start you see his improvement and the way his action had changed to compensate for his back problems.'

Australia was 6–259 at stumps on the first day, Boon contributing 48 and Border 73.

'AB made an excellent 70 at a time when some people were saying that he was losing his touch. The word was the West Indies would sort out whether he could still cope – there was no better answer for that on day one of the series,' Boon said.

Australia closed at 293 the following morning and West Indies had replied with 3–170 when the biggest controversy of the series erupted – Brian Lara stumped by Ian Healy off the bowling of Greg Matthews for 58, the dismissal adjudged by square-leg umpire Terry Prue. Television replays clearly showed that the Australian wicket-keeper had taken the bails off with his right glove, but without the ball.

Lara had gone down the wicket to Matthews, Healy had fumbled the ball on the leg-side, vainly trying to sweep it into the stumps. The confusion arose over whether he had the ball in his glove when the bails were dislodged.

'I was at cover, reasonably straight, so my view of the incident was somewhat restricted as to the ball's position,' Boon admitted.

'But running into the stumps, I could clearly hear what was being said. Lara had had two goes getting back into his crease and had slipped over. The television replays showed that the ball wasn't in the glove and had been knocked past the stumps when the glove went through them. But Healy throughout the whole business kept saying, "I don't know; I'm unsure".' Unfortunately, umpire Prue was emphatic about Lara being out.

Lara came into the Australian dressing room that night and shared a drink with his opponents.

'We all watched the replays and had a laugh. But the idea of a war between Australia and West Indies had started again. The whole summer, some sections of the media tried to pump up this issue. Sure, it was war on the field, like any Test series, but off the field there was no animosity.'

Lara's partner, Keith Arthurton, finished the evening on 61 not out and went on to post his maiden Test century, 157 not out, the next day.

Boon said that the Australians regarded both Lara and Arthurton as players confident in their own ability, but acknowledged that their ability was real.

Boon, from Australia's island State, Tasmania, could relate to Arthurton's pride in his own small island home, St Nevis, which had produced only two other Test cricketers, spinners Elquemedo Willett and Derek Parry.

The West Indies made 371, a lead of seventy-eight. Australia was unbeaten at 0–21 when stumps were drawn, but Boon said the final 30-odd minutes of play were horrendous from his perspective.

'Curtly Ambrose probably bowled the quickest he bowled for the entire series. I got to face the last over because Tubby had, fortuitously for him, rotated the strike in the previous over. On the third or fourth ball, umpire Prue no-balled Curtly! I said to myself, out loud, "Geez, Terry, don't do that at this time of night!" – or words to that effect.

'Phil Simmons was fielding at bat-pad and he just cracked up. Being an fellow opener, he knew what I was feeling, but his giggling beneath his helmet didn't help the situation.'

Boon started the fourth day on six, a score from which he immediately profited in Ambrose's first over – dropped at second slip by Carl Hooper. He made the West Indies pay, scoring 111 runs – his fourteenth Test century – including 13 boundaries in 325 minutes from 259 deliveries.

'I felt solid in my first dig and after my life in the second innings, didn't feel too bad; my confidence started to lift the longer I was in there and I started to play my shots more regularly,' Boon said.

'It was my third hundred against the West Indies, after 109 in the first Test in Jamaica (1991) and 149 in Sydney the series before that (1988–89). Every time you score a hundred against West Indies you know you've worked hard.'

Australia was 6–266 when play re-started on the final morning and were all out 308, setting the West Indies a target of 231 from a minimum of 65 overs.

The West Indies collapsed to be 3–3 at lunch and slumped further to be 4–9, six runs of which had come from a massive Richie Richardson hit over the fence off left-armer Bruce Reid.

Craig McDermott claimed Desmond Haynes (1), Brian Lara (0) and Keith Arthurton (0) to have figures of 3–3. Reid chipped in with Phil Simmons' wicket for one in that momentous 4.3 overs before the main interval.

Richardson then clouted the Australian bowling for 66 runs, surviving several close lbw appeals. Australians Allan Border and Merv Hughes were reported for dissent over an incident arising out of these appeals. The West Indies finished at 8–133 and the first Test was drawn.

Boon has never denied that comments are made out of frustration as players seek to establish an edge, particularly when a fielding side heckles a batsman, especially when there's a Test victory on the line.

Border, who didn't appear at the hearing – later admitting that he should have – was fined $2000 and Hughes $400 as penalty.

In the fifth and final Test in Perth, Border and Hughes were again carpeted.

For the entire summer, only the two Australians – and West Indian opener Desmond Haynes, who showed public dissent after being dismissed in a one-day game – were fined.

Boon himself, as Australia's acting-vice-captain with Mark Taylor omitted from the XI, attended the Perth hearing.

Australia began its campaign for the second Test of the series by making two changes to its starting 12 – one compulsory, the other by choice.

Left-arm paceman Bruce Reid injured his shoulder in the Sheffield Shield match against Victoria which followed the first Test, and was replaced by New South Wales leftie Mike Whitney. Dean Jones was omitted from the twelve itself, a victim of three first-class innings which had yielded only nine, 14 and one. His Victorian team-mate and leg-spinner Shane Warne returned to Test cricket following his spasmodic tour of Sri Lanka.

Australia batted first on a slow Melbourne Cricket Ground wicket, which had received limited preparation due to constant bad weather. Boon made 46, taking his Test run tally to precisely 1000 against the West Indies.

Just prior to lunch Boon shared an interesting moment with Steve Waugh, who made 38 in their second-wicket partnership of 62.

'It was about 10 minutes before lunch and Stephen backed away to leg and absolutely belted one through cover to the fence. I walked up the wicket and asked, innocently, "What are you doing?"

'He said, "I'm just going to be really positive."

'I said, "Can't you be really positive after lunch, rather than with 10 minutes to go?" He answered my question with a question, saying, '"Does it matter if you do it before or afterwards?"

'Through the series, Mark Waugh did it continually and Stephen occasionally. While it's not the way I play, those two have so much talent they tend to get away with it.'

At stumps, Australia was 4–227, with Mark Waugh (63) and Allan Border (51) undefeated.

After play, the Australian players were able to let coach Bob Simpson know that his Test record had been 'got'. When Boon reached twelve, he climbed to eighth on the all-time Australian batting list with 4870 runs, passing Simpson's total of 4869.

Border and Waugh, who shared a 204-run partnership for fifth wicket, directed Australia to a first innings total of 395. Border scored 110, his twenty-fifth Test century, eclipsing Greg Chappell and Viv Richards, who each posted twenty-four hundreds during their distinguished careers.

Mark Waugh's 112, his third Test century, saw him backing away to the West Indies' paceman with near-disastrous and occasionally comic results.

'At one stage, "Junior" (Mark Waugh) backed away outside leg stump and David Williams, the wicketkeeper, followed the ball. Waugh clipped the ball between the 'keeper and first slip – a gap of about 10 metres – for four! Williams had one of those games you have nightmares about – he scored a pair and dropped about four catches,' Boon said.

Merv Hughes then seized a further advantage by claiming three West Indian wickets – Desmond Haynes, Phil Simmons and Richie Richardson – as the tourists slumped to 3–62 at stumps.

Despite Brian Lara and Keith Arthurton putting on 106 for the fourth wicket, the West Indies were all out for 233. Australia led by 162 runs.

In Australia's second innings, Boon suffered an ignominious end on twelve, when medium-pacer Phil Simmons attempted to bounce him only to see the ball shot underneath Boon's bat in classic grubber style to bowl the disbelieving opener.

Australia was 1–26 at the end of the third day and all out 196 on the fourth. The West Indies needed 359 for victory from a minimum 103 overs. When the final morning dawned, West Indies were 1–32, requiring 327 runs in three sessions. History shows that West Indies didn't come close. What happened was 'The Warne Show'.

Warne, the blonde leg-spinner who had shed 15-odd kilograms over winter, finished the day with 7–52 from 23.2 overs – his final 14.4 overs yielding an incredible 7–21. He became the first leg-spinner to take five wickets at the MCG since the legendary Bill O'Reilly in 1936–37.

Warne's momentous afternoon began when he bowled captain Richie Richardson for 52; as the West Indies' skipper departed, the score was 2–143. Brian Lara soon followed, caught Boon, bowled Mike Whitney, at 3–148.

Warne claimed the next two wickets, Keith Arthurton stumped by Ian Healy and Carl Hooper caught by Whitney running in from the deep as the right-hander attempted to hit over the infield.

Craig McDermott chipped in to claim Jimmy Adams, caught at first slip by Mark Taylor.

The last three wickets – David Williams (0), Ian Bishop (7) and Courtney Walsh (0) – went to Warne. Walsh tried another big hit, but found the bigger hands of Merv Hughes, running around from mid-off. Hughes caught the ball and raced to the wicket to envelop his Victorian team-mate in his trademark bearhug, picking up a commemorative stump at the same time.

'In a way, that was Warne's turning-point as a Test cricketer,' Boon said. 'Since then, he's bowled well – in the majority of the Test series against West Indies and again in New Zealand.

'He's a different bowler to when he made his debut in Sydney against India and on tour in Sri Lanka. There, AB really had to look when to bowl him, and while he took three wickets at the end of the first Test in Colombo, he didn't bowl well on tour.'

Boon said that Warne definitely benefited from the MCG wicket and playing in front of his home crowd. 'But he's also improved as a bowler. He's bowling his wrong-'un more, his control and variation in flight has improved with the confidence he's earned. He's got a long way to go, but he will be a good bowler for a long time to come.'

Leaving Melbourne for the third Test in Sydney, Boon said that members of the Australian team reflected that in the past four Test matches at the MCG, Australia hadn't lost a match there, beating Pakistan in 1989–90, England in 1990–91 and India in 1991–92.

So it was a psychological turn-around to best the cricketers from the Caribbean in the surrounds of Australia's most revered sporting arena.

'We went to the Sydney Test with a degree of confidence, one-up after two matches,' Boon said. 'In the previous couple of series against West Indies, we had been two-down or more and pushing it uphill. It felt completely different to those of us who had played the Windies before.'

In the previous two series between Australia and the West Indies the Caribbean team had won 3–1 each time. The solitary blemish on each tour had occurred at the Sydney Cricket Ground, and each time the main destroyer for Australia had been a spinner: Bob Holland in '84–85 and Allan Border in '88–89.

The condition of the wicket for the third Test at the Sydney Cricket Ground this time around could be described in one word: flat. Understandably, the West Indies' pacemen and management were a tad miffed; Australia, however, with two spinners – Shane Warne and Greg Matthews – in the team, were eager for the contest to begin.

However, the problem was, that apart from being flat, the wicket didn't spin.

'There was some grass, but no turn, like a normal Sydney deck,' Boon said.

Australia won the toss and batted first for the third time in the series. Boon scored 76, continuing his substantial plundering of runs in Sydney.

Steve Waugh, who, batting at number three now as Boon was opening, had been criticised for his technique against the short ball in the Test matches in Brisbane and Melbourne. He responded to the pressure with a century. After acknowledging the crowd, who rose as one to salute their fellow New South Welshman, Waugh sent a less than subtle signal to the press box.

'Stephen got a hundred and played really well, plus he got a few people off his back,' Boon commented.

However, long-time commentators of the game, including distinguished ex-players, had focused on his penchant for playing back-foot drives – with which he destroyed the English bowlers and received rare praise indeed – against West Indies' unforgiving pace, declaring the technique suspect. Even his century in Sydney was downplayed because of the wicket conditions.

Australia amassed 503 runs in its first innings, but even that total was eclipsed by Allan Border completing an epic journey to become only the second player in the history of Test cricket to reach 10,000 runs. He needed 21 runs at the start of the Test to join Indian master batsman Sunil Gavaskar on this magical figure. The left-hander, New South Wales-born but Queensland-adopted, spent nine minutes and nine balls on 9,999 runs. But at 12.09 pm on 3 January 1993, Border, in his 136th Test match, bunted off-spinner Carl Hooper for a single for his 10,000.

West Indies was 1–32 when play closed on the second day. But if the SCG crowd had been witness to Border's achievement, another left-hander was to make the hallowed oval come alive again. When rain stopped play at 5.13 pm on day three, Brian Lara was 121 not out, having shared an unbroken partnership of 217 with his captain, Richie Richardson.

The 23-year-old Trinidadian finished his maiden Test century with a total of 277, only 88 behind Sir Garfield Sobers' all-time record Test score of 365 not out.

'Lara's 277, his first Test century, was obviously talked about by the players afterwards,' Boon said. 'He got in, and he's obviously a very good player, but we couldn't remember him hitting the field. For his total innings, every time he hit the ball hard, it hit the gap and went for four. And he would have scored more but for a shocking mix-up with Carl Hooper.'

Lara had given a chance on 172, Steve Waugh missing him in the gully, but seemed nigh-unstoppable until he pushed Greg Matthews to cover and called a single to Hooper, who didn't respond. Damien Martyn's throw to Ian Healy found Lara short of his ground.

The West Indies made 606, outscoring Australia on the first innings for the second time in the series Australia was 0–117 in its second innings when the match closed a draw, meaningful for both Boon and his country. Boon and Mark Taylor's unbeaten opening stand was a record against West Indies at the SCG.

More significantly, Boon, who finished 63 not out, passed 5000 Test runs when he reached nine; on 22, he scored his 1000th Test run in Sydney. Boon became the third highest Australian Test run-maker against the West Indies at the SCG, behind Greg Chappell (1150) and his own captain, Border (1121).

'I was definitely counting those nine runs,' Boon said. 'For some reason, because I like playing in Sydney and I have had success on this ground, I wanted my 5000th run to come at the SCG.'

Damien Martyn was the first Australian player injured in the events surrounding the fourth Test, but he sustained his injury before a ball had been bowled.

The Australians were training as usual the day before the Test began. Martyn, an exuberant and talented young man playing his first series, had returned the ball to Australian coach Bob Simpson.

'Simmo dropped it,' Boon recalled. 'Being in an enthusiastic mood,

Marto ran in flat out to pick it up. Simmo, not knowing Damien was sprinting in, picked the ball up and threw his hands out to signal the end of the session – Marto ran straight into his outstretched thumb.'

The 20-year-old Martyn was hospitalised immediately after Australian physiotherapist Errol Alcott assessed the injury. Martyn suffered acute bleeding behind his left eye and was placed in a darkened room for four days.

Into Martyn's place, the Australian selectors called on his Western Australian team-mate Justin Langer to make his Test debut.

For the first time in the series, Australian captain Allan Border lost the toss and the West Indian captain Richie Richardson decided, understandably, to bat first on the Adelaide wicket, traditionally a batsman's track.

Cruising at 0–84, West Indies slumped to be all out for 252 as Merv Hughes claimed 5–64 from only 21.3 overs. Desmond Haynes (45) and Phil Simmons (46) batted well, but the only other contributions came from Brian Lara (52) and 'keeper Junior Murray (49). The possibility of winning the series glimmered on the horizon for an Australian team which had suffered so many disappointments at the hands of their Caribbean counterparts.

But once again, the West Indies' pace attack extracted the highest price on Australia's batsmen.

Ian Bishop had Mark Taylor caught in slips for only one run in the right-hander's first over. His dismissal brought Langer to the wicket for the first time in a Test match. The headlines screamed 'Baptism of Fire for Langer' the next day, but the cliche rang grimly realistic. Facing only his fourth ball, he was struck in the head by a sharply rising delivery from Ian Bishop. Such was the pace it cracked the back of Langer's new protective head gear.

Langer suffered a cut to the back of his head and an enormous headache, but his courage won the instant admiration of his team-mates and the rest of the cricketing world.

'Langer is a gutsy little bloke – he's got a lot of grit in him,' Boon said. 'To make getting hit in the head worse, he'd suffered concussion after getting pinged the week before, fielding at bat-pad for Western Australia.'

Boon had offered the usual words of advice to Langer, who holds a black belt in the martial art of Tae Kwon Do, and was again surprised by his new batting partner's response to the situation.

'I said to him, "Get in there behind it, keep talking and watching the ball." But he wasn't just content with that; he kept telling me what to do, kept encouraging me!

'I got a bit annoyed when, with Bishop running in, Langer pulled away because he suffered some blurred vision and several West Indians, fielding close to the wicket, hopped straight into him. I just told him that if his vision was blurred, to take his time before facing again.'

Langer and Boon had taken Australia's total to two without further loss when bad light closed play.

Boon himself was the next man injured, struck in the elbow by Curtly Ambrose.

For years, commentators have described Boon as 'tough as teak', perhaps overdoing the cliches in a bid to capture the essence of his legendary courage and talent for being unfazed under extreme physical pressure. Boon himself has often said that when hit by a bowler, a batsman should try to exhibit no visible pain – while acknowledging that this can be almost impossible, especially when a finger gets jammed between bat handle and ball, or a broken digit is struck again.

But this was different – Boon was in absolute agony, dropping his bat and staggering around the wicket, unable even to be held still by concerned West Indian cricketers, such was the pain.

ABC cricket commentator Neville Oliver was on-air at the time and made mention of the fact that after Boon was struck, he began to limp markedly. The Australian opener had been playing with a hamstring strain, one which he had disguised. But as his body reacted to the massive damage to his arm, his leg became vulnerable and exposed.

For his team-mates, opponents and cricket fans watching the game live or on television, it was a heart-wrenching and sickening period of time. Boon had almost assuredly suffered major injury and in those first few moments, thoughts arose of a broken elbow, radius or ulna bones which might require the insertion of a plate or pins, immobilising the arm and his career. For the first time in his Test career, Boon was forced to retire hurt.

'I thought it was going to bounce more, but when I realised it wasn't going to, I tried to get out of the way. But it was going so quickly I couldn't. I didn't hear anything, I only felt it.

'I was lucky in a way, because the ball actually hit me an inch or two below the elbow,' Boon said.

'The worrying thing was that when Errol Alcott and the doctor came out to the middle, I couldn't move my hand and they kept asking me if I had any feeling in my little finger. My hand was completely numb down the side which goes to the little finger and I was told later that this was an indication that the arm was broken.'

Fortunately – or perhaps a better description would be miraculously – x-rays cleared Boon of major damage.

'When the doctor told me there was no break, he said, "If that doesn't break your arm, you'll have to get hit by a train to break it,"' Boon said. 'I said thanks very much.'

'A similar thing happened to me in England, when I was hit in the left hand in a County game. It now feels like the bone is sort of bent, there's a depression in the bone below the elbow.'

While Boon might not have heard the impact on his elbow, his team-mates – when they knew he was relatively undamaged – told him of the sound echoing across the Adelaide Oval.

Boon had retired hurt on two and Australia was 3-100 at stumps, Steve Waugh not out 35 and Allan Border unbeaten on 18.

Returning from hospital, Boon found he couldn't move the arm, so he asked Alcott to treat it. 'Hooter' did so willingly, creating even more agony for his friend. 'I was scared that after trying to keep it moving, it would seize up overnight,' Boon said. 'But the next morning, it was okay, I was able to go swimming.'

'When I went out to bat again, I wore an arm guard for the first time. But the problem was that I didn't have any strength in my top hand and I couldn't get my elbow up. I certainly got a work-out to see how the elbow was going! But no matter who Australia was playing, I knew that that would be the reaction.'

Australia was bundled out for 213, Steve Waugh making 42 and Merv Hughes belting 43; Boon was unbeaten on 39 – Ambrose was the destroyer, a definite omen, capturing 6–74.

But again this incredible match turned, as the West Indies were dismissed for a mere 146 in the second innings, leaving Australia a target of 186 to win the Sir Frank Worrell Trophy.

South Australian off-spinner Tim May, recalled to Test cricket for the first time in four years, captured an amazing haul of 5–9 from 6.5 overs. In fact, May claimed 5–5 from 32 deliveries as the last six West Indian wickets fell for only 22 runs in 39 minutes.

May has been plagued by chronic injury problems – the previous season, 1991–92, he needed his twelfth knee operation to get onto the field – and poor form, which began on the 1989 Ashes tour of England.

May took the wickets of Carl Hooper (25), Junior Murray (0), Ian Bishop (6), Ambrose (1) and Kenneth Benjamin (0).

Shane Warne provided the vital wicket of Richie Richardson, tempting the West Indies' skipper down the wicket to be caught behind by Ian Healy.

Australia hadn't held the hallowed Worrell trophy since 1975–76, but it was now tantalisingly within reach, if only Ambrose could be defied.

No one anticipated what was to happen on the final day in Ade-laide, a day of drama, ecstasy and agony for the cricketing public that kept an entire country clustered around radio and television sets.

Ambrose began the day by sending Boon back to the pavilion for a duck in his third over. Then Benjamin had Mark Taylor caught behind for seven and Mark Waugh was caught by Hooper off the bowling of Bishop for 26; Australia was an uneasy 3–64 at lunch.

First ball after the interval, Ambrose took Steve Waugh's wicket – driving a ball to Keith Arthurton at cover. Border received a brutish short ball, to which he could do nothing more than pop a catch to Desmond Haynes at short leg. Hughes was trapped leg before wicket to give Ambrose his tenth wicket for the match. Australia was finished, 7–74.

Into that chasm stepped Justin Langer, who combined with first Warne and then May to take the score to 9–144. Warne batted for 72 invaluable minutes for nine; Langer, who was caught behind by Murray off Bishop for 54, and May put on 42 for the ninth wicket.

This left May at the wicket, joined by Craig McDermott, the bowler whose batting against genuine pace had gone downhill since he was struck in the head by Courtney Walsh in Jamaica in 1991.

'Maysie gets terrorised in the nets when our blokes are bowling to him. Especially Steve and Mark Waugh – they're always peppering him with short balls,' Boon, explaining the mammoth task confronting the Australian pair against the best bowling side in the world which needed only one wicket to level the series.

'But Craig kept hanging in there, staying in line, which he hadn't done since being hit in West Indies. Really, for two years, he'd been backing away. This was really good for him, because it gave him back his confidence with his batting.'

May and McDermott added 40 runs in 88 minutes to take Australia through to 9–186, only one run short of a tied Test match and two runs away from a series victory.

'Nobody had moved in the dressing-room. Everyone had kept the same seats,' said Boon, describing the Australian team's superstition in times of pressure.

'There were plenty of sweating hands, but there was no real panic, Every ball it was, "Well done, Billy (McDermott)" or shouts for Maysie scoring runs.'

On the last ball of the seventy-ninth over, Courtney Walsh dug one in short. McDermott tried to avoid it. There was a deflection, a sound – but from where or what piece of equipment was unclear, even with repeated television replays – but umpire Darrell Hair's finger was raised.

Australia was all out for 186. The West Indies had won the Test match by one solitary run and the series was level at 1–1.

'Everyone just sat there in silence,' Boon, even now his voice tinged with depression and awe of the situation. 'To get that close, we weren't expecting that. But the last decision – it was one of those magnificent decisions, because the ball hit the front of Craig's helmet grille and then glanced off the wrist of his glove.

'It was like when Steve Randell made his first decision in one-day international cricket, giving Javed Miandad out, run out by a centimetre.'

May was 42 not out; McDermott made 18 runs.

On the humorous side of cricket, Boon said that May's now-legendary description of his innings almost defies repetition – because it's being regularly embellished.

'First he loses an eye, then the quadricep muscle in his left knee is collapsed because he's hit in the pad so much. The doctors sew his eye back, but his arm gets knocked off, so then he's batting one-handed,' Boon laughs.

However, Boon also states that because of the emotional roller-coaster of the final session, coupled with the end result of losing the match, this Test in Adelaide has become one of the lowlights of his career. But for two runs, Australia would have been acclaimed world champion for beating West Indies 2–0. Now it was one all and with the final Test in Perth, anything was possible.

For David Boon, the Perth wicket prepared for the final Test was one of the quickest in his experience. Curtly Ambrose, unfortunately, proved Boon correct, taking 7–25 to dismiss Australia for only 119. In fact, Ambrose took 7–1 from 32 balls, an incredible haul, but one which the 29-year-old Antiguan had threatened to reap all summer.

By doing so, Ambrose equalled Joel Garner's record of 31 wickets in a series by a West Indian against Australia, set in the Caribbean in 1983–84.

Boon top-scored in Australia's innings with 44, but he too was one of Ambrose's victims.

Ambrose's day was constructed thus: at 2–85 he had Mark Waugh caught behind for nine by Junior Murray, from the fourth ball of his twelfth over. His figures were 1–22. At 3–90 David Boon was caught at gully by Richie Richardson from the fifth ball of Ambrose's thirteenth over: 3–22. At 4–90 Allan Border was caught behind by Murray for a first-ball duck from Ambrose's next ball: 3–22 (three wickets for no runs in nine balls). At 5–100 Ian Healy was caught at first slip for a duck by Brian Lara from the fourth ball of Ambrose's fifteenth over: 4–23 (four wickets for one run in 19 balls). At 6–102 Merv Hughes was caught at cover for a duck by Keith Arthurton from the second ball of Ambrose's sixteenth over: 5–23 (five wickets for one run from 23 balls). At 7–104 Damien Martyn edged the ball to Phil Simmons at second slip for 13 from the first ball of Ambrose's seventeenth over: 6–23 (six wickets for one run in 28 balls). At 8–104 newcomer Jo Angel was caught behind for a duck by Murray from the fifth ball of the same over: 7–23 (seven wickets for one run in 23 balls).

'The wicket suited the West Indies' bowling down to the ground,' was Boon's dry comment.

Pakistan's Sarfraz Nawaz took 7–1 in 33 balls as Australia was bowled out for 310 at the Melbourne Cricket Ground in 1978–79. He finished with 9–86 as Australia went from 3–305 to 310 all out.

West Indies made 322 in their first innings, Phil Simmons top-scoring with 80. Keith Arthurton made 77, Richie Richardson 47 and Junior Murray 37; Merv Hughes took 4–71, taking his series' total to 20 wickets.

At stumps on day two, Australia was again reeling at 4–75, still trailing by 122 runs overall.

Boon was undefeated on 45 after the loss of Justin Langer (1),

Steve Waugh (0), Mark Waugh (21) and Shane Warne (0). Damien Martyn, on three, was with Boon.

Australian vice-captain Mark Taylor had been omitted from the final match, Boon opening with Langer.

The initial breakthrough was made by Ambrose, as expected, when Langer was caught at gully by substitute fieldsman Gus Logie with the total at 13. Australia was 2-14 when Steve Waugh fended a short ball to Logie, again at gully.

Boon and Mark Waugh added 52 runs for the third wicket, before Waugh was dismissed just before the close of play – attempting to withdraw the bat against Bishop, but deciding at the last moment to play a shot, guiding the ball to Richardson at third slip.

Warne, Australia's newest nightwatchman, lasted only two balls, edging Ambrose to Murray. This gave Ambrose 33 wickets, equalling the record for a series held by Clarrie Grimmett (1930–31) and Alan Davidson (1960–61).

On the third day of the Test, Australia was all out for 178 in its second innings, a defeat by an innings and 25 runs.

Ian Bishop forestalled Ambrose's chance to break the record by adding four more wickets to his overnight tally of two to finish with 6–40. Ambrose didn't get another chance.

Boon again top-scored with 52 and Healy (27) and Hughes (22) showed some resistance to the inevitable.

The West Indies had won the series 2–1, maintaining the winning record that has stood since 1975–76. Ambrose won the Man of the Match, Man of the Series and International Cricketer of the Year awards – including a $52,000 four-wheel-drive car.

One of the most ebullient images of the series was Ambrose behind the wheel of his prize, with his team-mates crammed into, onto and hanging off the sides of the car for a victory lap, and given a rousing reception by the Perth crowd.

Boon is the first to acknowledge the brilliance of Ambrose.

'Curtly was the difference between the two sides. They got into a position to win in Adelaide, and despite the fact that we fought back, they won. We had three opportunities to win – in Brisbane, where we couldn't wrap it up on the last day, in Melbourne where we won and in Adelaide, where we failed by two runs. They had two opportunities, Adelaide and Perth, and they won both of them.

'Curtly was the key to so much of what they did. Before the series and again before the Perth Test, Michael Holding stated that, in his opinion, Ambrose was just outside the highest echelon of West Indian quicks. After the Perth Test, Michael said that Curtly was one of the best.'

Boon said that Ambrose rarely bowled a 'technical' bouncer, concentrating on the area between a batsman's throat and hip, the secret to his success.

Since 1988–89, when Ambrose debuted in Australia, Boon has enjoyed, if enjoyment is a correct description, their contests between bat and ball. And after winning the series, Ambrose opened up as a person, as opposed to his usual taciturn mien.

'I remember sitting at a dinner table with Curtly in the West Indies and he didn't say anything. He would always say hello, but that was about it. But after this match, we had a chat for 15 minutes or so in the West Indian dressing rooms. Kenneth Benjamin was having problems with his knee and Curtly said that it was because 'Benjy' was too heavy. Curtly said: "He should be built like a gazelle. Like me."'

AWAY: VERSUS NEW ZEALAND

For David Boon, the three-Test tour of New Zealand will always be remembered as a time of sadness, because before the first warm-up game against a New Zealand Board XI in New Plymouth, he had to return home because of the death of his father, Clarrie. Boon flew home to attend his father's funeral and returned to New Zealand for the first Test match at Christchurch.

The build-up to the first Test in Christchurch in late February was overshadowed by the likelihood of Australian captain Allan Border scoring the 50 runs needed to become the leading run-scorer in Test history. Interestingly, Border had scored a pair in the final Test against West Indies in Perth. And in the first tour game in New Zealand, at New Plymouth, the Queenslander suffered another nought.

However, the Lancaster Park wicket set before the two teams glistened with promise for their respective fast bowlers. New Zealand won the toss and, understandably, sent Australia into bat.

'There had been a lot of rain in the lead-up to the Test and the wicket was grassy, with much more grass on it than normal,' David Boon said. 'We would have done exactly the same thing if we'd won the toss.'

Boon made only 15 runs, but was at the crease for more than an hour, as the wicket seamed and the ball swung as expected, but the New Zealand pace attack was unable to take advantage of the conditions.

'Mark Taylor and I had a quite a lengthy start and then he and Justin Langer batted through. Their bowlers just bowled too wide. I remember thinking at the time, God help us if Sir Richard Hadlee had been playing! We'd have been playing at nine out of 10 deliveries instead of letting seven out of 10 go.'

Taylor made 82 and Langer (63 not out) and Steve Waugh (33 not out) batted through to see Australia to a comfortable 4–217 at the close of play.

Day two belonged to Border. In his 139th Test match, he took 160 minutes to compile the 50 runs to surpass Sunil Gavaskar on 10,122 runs. At the end of his innings, Border had scored 88.

'When he broke the record, it wasn't done in what you'd call classical fashion,' Boon said. He came down the wicket to what looked like an arm ball from Dipak Patel. But rather than get down to it, he played an upright sweep shot and the ball was in the air for a long, long time! Chris Cairns was fielding at backward square and we were concerned that he was going to gobble it up. But he just jogged around – we were quite amazed.'

Boon was unstinting in his praise and pride in his friend and skipper becoming the new Test record-holder. 'To me, it's just desserts for somebody who has given so much to the game, played for so long and given so much to Australian cricket. Looking at the batting list, he's going to be the record-holder for quite some time because no one is in a position at the moment to break his record.'

The Australian team celebrated with a big, engraved cake – thankfully not with a candle for each run – and a special commemorative photograph to mark his achievement.

Australia made 485 in total, Steve Waugh with 62, Ian Healy 54 and Merv Hughes a big-hitting 45.

New Zealand was 2–30 overnight, but collapsed to be all out for 182 and forced to follow-on. At stumps on the third day, the Kiwis were 3–37, still 266 in arrears with two days remaining.

Australia achieved victory by an innings and 60 runs by dismissing New Zealand for 263, in which Ken Rutherford scored 102 and Murphy Su'a 44; Merv Hughes and Shane Warne each took four wickets.

'Our thrashing New Zealand was absolutely huge in their media, who were saying that there would have to be a lot of soul-searching and changes for them to come back in a three-Test series,' Boon said. 'Martin Crowe apparently offered to resign, which made the controversy surrounding their defeat even bigger. But we were talking about the fact that New Zealand would come back and fight hard, because Australia has a lot of memories of them doing just that.'

On the first day of the second Test at Wellington's Basin Reserve only 12.1 overs were possible because of poor weather and New Zealand was 0–28 when play was abandoned.

Day two saw New Zealand bat stubbornly, led by veteran John Wright, who made 72 in six hours – posting a 111-run opening stand with Mark Greatbatch (61) – before skipper Martin Crowe opened up.

Crowe was 62 overnight and went on to make 97, with some accidental intervention by Boon himself, much to the annoyance of Merv Hughes.

'I was fielding at third man when Crowe was batting and he played a cut shot. I went haring around the boundary which is marked by a chalk line inside the fence. I stuck my foot out to stop the ball and pinged it back in, while they ran three,' Boon said. 'But the television replays showed that the ball had crossed the chalk line, although I had no idea at the time. Crowe had 96 on the board, but the next morning when we got up, he had 97 and Merv Hughes's figures had gone from 3–99 to 3–100. He was very unimpressed.

'What we found interesting was that if Crowe's shot was a four, he would have been at the other end and the batting should have been changed around. That was the first time we could remember a batsman's score being changed like that.'

New Zealand made 329, to which Australia replied with 298, Kiwi paceman Danny Morrison posting career-best figures of 7–89 from 26.4 overs, including an eight-over spell which realised 6–38. Morrison trapped Border lbw for 30 in the first over with the new ball and followed that with Ian Healy (8), Hughes (8), Paul Reiffel (7), Steve Waugh (75) and Warne (22).

The match finished in a draw with New Zealand 7–210 in its second innings.

Allan Border's last-minute change of mind to bat at Auckland's Eden Park in the third Test after winning the toss proved disastrous for Australia. At the close of play on the first day they had struggled to 9–139 after having been 6–48 at one stage.

David Boon made 20, Steve Waugh top-scored with 41 and Merv Hughes 33 on the first day, but lost the final wicket the next morning without further addition.

New Zealand answered with 224. Hughes took 3–67 and Warne 4–8 from 15 overs, including 12 maidens. In doing so, the Victorian leg-spinner equalled Dennis Lillee's Australian record of 15 wickets in a series in New Zealand, set in 1976–77.

Australia again slumped to be 4–119 in its second innings, rescued by Border's 61 not out to be 6–226 at stumps. Australia was all out for 285, setting New Zealand a target of 201 to level the series and retain the Trans-Tasman Trophy.

New Zealand was 5–168 when play closed on the fourth day, but needed only 29 minutes the next morning to post the necessary 33 runs for no further loss, Ken Rutherford finishing with 53 not out.

This match also marked the retirement from Test cricket of New Zealand opener John Wright, for whom Boon has nothing but respect.

'John has become a good mate over the time I've played cricket against New Zealand. I've always found him similar to me, in that he calls a spade a spade and once play was over he always enjoyed associating with his opponents,' Boon said. 'Wright was always the first one in to the Australian dressing room when it was their turn to have drinks with us – quite often, he was the only one!'

Boon and the rest of the Australians avoided, as much as possible, the controversy that raged in New Zealand through the series, revolving around captain Martin Crowe.

'We read about the Crowe controversy and found it very humorous. In fact, we talked about it to Crowe after the day's play was over,' Boon said. 'The New Zealand media were putting so much pressure on the poor bloke. They insinuated his wife should go and he should stay, when he threatened to resign after the loss in the first Test.'

In the second Test in Wellington, Crowe confronted several New Zealand journalists before a press conference began, regarding allegations about his sexuality.

'All credit to Crowe because he stood up for what he believed in, stood up for his pride and his family to some very cruel accusations,' Boon said.

However, Boon admitted he was surprised by the New Zealand team's reaction to Wright's last Test.

'Myself, AB and some of the young blokes went in to have drink with Wrightie and there were more of us in their dressing-room than New Zealanders,' Boon said. 'We found it amazing, because Australia treats victory, treats everything, as a team. New Zealand had just retained the Trans-Tasman Trophy and their most senior players was retiring – but the majority of their players didn't stay around. I thought John Wright deserved more.

'I know that there were huge accolades from the media and public and special presentations to Wright after the game, but he deserved more from his peers.'

Boon said that Wright provided him, fielding at bat-pad in New Zealand's first innings, with another humorous sidelight.

'Wright is a gutsy sort of player who never gives anything away. But he talks to himself, like a lot of batsmen, and that can be pretty funny to listen to,' Boon said. 'When he was still on nought, he slashed at one and it went over the top of slips for four. Wrightie said, "Thank Christ for that – now I can't get a pair in my last Test!"'

5
BOON'S
VIEWS

MALCOLM MARSHALL AND MY FIRST TEST

'My first experience of Malcolm Marshall was in the first-ever Test I played for Australla, in Brisbane against West Indies in 1984–85. Australia had been absolutely thrashed in the first Test in Perth. That was the game in which my favourite Rodney Hogg story occurred.

Hoggie, like my Dad, must have every Test match he's played video-ed in full, so that his children could watch in years to come. But in Perth, Rodney was guilty of a horrific retreat from the batting crease in the face of Michael Holding's bowling. But Michael's aim followed him with the ball and Hogg was hit on the pad, more than a metre outside leg-stump, and the ball ricocheted onto the stumps and bowled him.

Hogg walked off the WACA Ground into the dressing rooms and

telephoned home. He told his wife to erase the video-tape: 'Because I don't want my son to know I was a coward,' was Hogg's honest comment.

My first Test was certainly an eventful one, the final game of Kim Hughes' Australian captaincy. Hughes resigned his position in Brisbane at the post-match media conference amid huge controversy.

But when the Test started, I had replaced Graham Yallop in the XII. Interestingly, it was Allan Border I sat next to in the Australian dressing room during my first match.

The Australian team then was completely different in personnel and attitude to what exists now. The current Australian team has the philosophy that the twelve players on the day are regarded as the nation's best. And, no matter how many Test matches you have under your belt, everyone's opinion counts, from the debut player to AB.

However, in my first game, I wasn't saying very much at all anyway. Allan offered me some sterling advice: 'If you want to say anything, make sure you're 200 per cent correct before you open your trap.'

When I ventured onto the 'Gabba in batting pads, the first ball I faced was delivered by Joel Garner. He tried the first-ball yorker, but my stature helped because his full-toss hit me shin-high.

I was batting with Border and the ball went out to Larry Gomes at mid-on. The single was on, but the call was somewhat bizarre: 'Yes! No! Wait! Sorry! Come back for two!' In the end I was almost run out from my first ball in Test cricket.

I made 12, edging my former Tasmanian team-mate Holding to Richie Richardson at second slip.

It was in the second innings that I first met Marshall on the Test arena. I had made a few runs but after a while Marshall, who was bowling fairly 'sharpish', trotted those extra few steps down from his follow-through and said: 'Boonie, I know that it's your first Test match but are you going to do the right thing and get out? Or do I have come around the wicket and kill you?' Being a shy young man at the time, I didn't say a word back – in fact, I'm not sure if I even looked at him. However, he was true to his word.

The problem with Marshall's bowling style was that when he came around the wicket, because of the angle of his run-up, you couldn't catch sight of him until he was in his delivery stride, right beside the umpire.

I was still in when Hogg came to the wicket. 'Babs,' he said, 'This is the perfect opportunity to start your career with a good average by a not out because I don't think I'm going to hang around too long!' But Hoggie did hang around and batted extremely well for a tail-order paceman.

It was during an over which Marshall bowled menacingly around the wicket that I hit the ball perfectly, hooking to the boundary. Hogg came storming down the wicket towards me in what I thought was experienced player – young player congratulation mode. However, instead of the pat on the back I was expecting, Hoggie shrieked, 'What do you think you're trying to do – get us all killed!'

That was probably Marshall's fastest series in Australia. In the West Indies in 1991, 'Turbo' had slowed a yard, but he still had the fearsome capability to remind you of his previous pace. And like Dennis Lillee, the great Australian paceman whose speed was restricted from all-out, flat-out because of back injuries, Marshall knew how to use the ball: the off-cutter, leg-cutter, in- and out-swinger. And it was all at a very, very good pace, just not only what's labelled 'tearaway'.

Marshall became very effective at exerting relentless pressure with line and length bowling, instead of just trying to blast batsmen out. I always enjoyed batting to him, but this extra mental game was very exciting and I was always very annoyed to be dismissed by him.

One of my major cricket philosophies is that what is said or happens on-field in the heat of the moment should stay there. Whatever the situation, Malcolm was one cricketer who always said hello before and after play. He was a player respected worldwide for his ability with the ball and as a dangerous bowler. He batted as high as six and could never be correctly tagged as part of the West Indies' tail-order.

I became Malcolm's 300th Test wicket – leg before wicket at the Melbourne Cricket Ground. Afterwards, he said to me, 'Bad luck!', because the decision was somewhat debatable.

But he still took the wicket!'

THE AUSTRALIA–WEST INDIES FEUD OF 1991

'My first Test series, against the West Indies in 1984-85, was characterised by a reasonable level of socialisation between the two teams. The second time I played Test cricket against the West Indies was 1988-89, the season in which Stephen Waugh went head-to-head with Patrick Patterson and Vivian Richards. Things had cooled by then. However, in the West Indies in 1991, the tour started without animosity, although it had been billed as the 'world championship' of cricket – Australia had come to take away the mantle.

Before the first Test in Jamaica, the managers and coaches convened and decided that a policy of sociability was in order. I thought the move was excellent, because I am a big believer that this plays a major part in the learning process of cricket. When I was a young batsman, I learnt so much about the game of cricket in that half-hour after play, swopping ideas, tactics, theories and yarns in the dressing room.

In Jamaica, things got off to a good start with the players meeting after the day's cricket in one or the other's dressing room. And on the first day's play in the second Test at Guyana, a few of the Australian players, including myself, went into the West Indian rooms. Unfortunately, on the second day, the West Indies fielded for the entire six hours and not one opposition player came to our rooms.

It just got worse from there. Australia's second innings in Guyana was marred irrevocably by Dean Jones's controversial run-out after he was bowled off a no-ball. Allan Border was extremely upset by the incident and the congeniality ended completely after that. Of course, the Australian players spoke to the West Indians. But the 'contracted to meet after every day's play for refreshment' – whether it be beer or mineral water – wasn't honoured.

It was during the fourth Test in Barbados that Australian wicketkeeper Ian Healy and West Indian opener Desmond Haynes re-opened major hostilities. I'm the first to admit that Healy is a typical 'keeper – aggressive to the point of distraction for opposing batsmen is a fair description. But Haynes is no shrinking violet. In fact, from personal experience, I rate him as an A-1 'baiter'.

It would also be wrong not to point out that Healy and Haynes, being the personalities they are, have no trouble trading insults. However, I do disagree with the fact that Haynes, after being dismissed, marched around to the media centre and complained about Healy's comments.

We once played a day-nighter in Sydney, Geoff Marsh and myself opening the batting and Curtly Ambrose and Malcolm Marshall the bowling. Roger Harper was fielding one side of the wicket and Gus Logie was the other. After eight overs, Australia had scored only eight runs and the crowd was getting somewhat restless. In a mid-wicket conversation, I mentioned to Marsh that the situation was 'pretty difficult'.

'Well, you're going to have to do something about it, aren't you?' was his reply.

Warm, caring, compassionate bloke, Swamp.

The next delivery was an in-swinger from Malcolm Marshall to me, which I picked up early and hit for six. Haynes who was fielding at mid-wicket called out, 'Isn't it great, Boonie, when you hit these supposed fast bowlers for six.' Malcolm's eyes just about rolled around in his head hearing that dig and thereafter he became very interested in ending my life, or at least putting holes in my body.

Back to Barbados – I have never denied that things are said on the cricket field of which players rightly feel ashamed. Again, I am of the opinion that what is said on-field in the heat of the moment stays there. However, the situation is not always one-way – a vile Australian bagging of a Sri Lankan (for example) is 'balanced' by a Pakistani warming to the subject in Urdu (or even Etonian English).

Another example of Australia–West Indies 'aggro', which ended unfortunately, was the last Test match in Perth in 1988–89. Curtly Ambrose hit New South Wales captain and tail-order batsman Geoff Lawson in the face, shattering his jaw. Australia declared immediately, and Border decided to utilise the team's heightened emotions to seek 'revenge' for a downed team-mate.

Merv Hughes is one cricketer who doesn't take much to get pumped up, and bowling the first ball of the West Indian innings, trapped Gordon Greenidge leg before wicket. In the resulting hullabaloo, Merv ran down the wicket, signalling and shouting to Greenidge that a shower was in order. Gordon was not amused and words were exchanged. After play finished for the day, Merv realised that he had over-reacted. At that time, Merv was in one of his 'non-drinking' phases, so he picked up a couple of stubbies of beer and two bottles of mineral water and went into the West Indies' room.

I was already there, talking to Jeff Dujon when Hughes entered, looking for Greenidge. Dujon said that the result would be 'very interesting'. Merv spotted Greenidge and approached him, proffering a beer and an apology for what had been said.

'I didn't mean it, I was just pumped up. If I offended you, I want to apologise,' Hughes said.

Gordon's reply was: 'You don't mean that,' and left the dressing room to sit in the team bus until the West Indians returned to their hotel.

It was after the Barbados Test in 1991 that West Indies' captain Viv Richards uttered his now-famous words about Australian coach Bob Simpson as a 'moaner and bad loser' in response

ABOVE: An early forcing stroke off the back foot as an opener for the Launceston Cricket Club under-16s, Invermay Park, 1974, aged 14 years.
(Photo: The Examiner)
BELOW: Aged three at Invermay Park, watching mum play hockey.

At the North Tasmanian Cricket Association ground, aged 17.

(Photo: The Examiner)

ABOVE: With parents Clarrie and Lesley Boon in the Australian dressing room after scoring 184 not out in the Bicentennial Test, Sydney, against England.
BELOW: Getting married in the chapel at my old school, Launceston Grammar, 30 April 1983.

(photo: The Examiner)

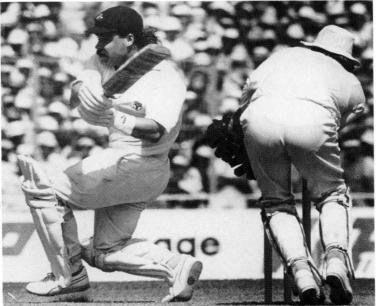

ABOVE: With Jack (one week old) and Georgina (three years two months).
(Photo: The Examiner)
BELOW: A pull shot that contributed to my Man-of-the-Match score of 75 in the 1987 World Cup Final against England at Eden Gardens, Calcutta. Paul Downton is the English wicketkeeper.
(Photo: Nikhil Bhattacharya)

ABOVE: The victorious Australian 1987 World Cup squad, Eden Gardens, Calcutta.

(Photo: Nikhil Bhattacharya)

BELOW: Man of the Match, a solid gold punchbowl, tray and goblets for 184 not out against England in the Bicentennial Test Match, Sydney 1988.

ABOVE: Four runs off Vic Marks at Lord's, 1989. Geoff Marsh and I put on a record one-day first-wicket stand (277) against the MCC XI.
(Photo: Rebecca Naden)
BELOW: Singing the song after clinching the Ashes at Old Trafford, 1989. (Champagne corks are part of a tradition in Lancashire.)
(Photo: Graham Morris)

On my way to 149 against the West Indies, Sydney Test, 1988-89.

ABOVE: 1990-91 World Series winning squad, victorious over New Zealand and England.

(Photo: Gregg Porteous)

BELOW: Versus England, Sydney, 1990-91.

ABOVE AND BELOW: The one that got away: Atherton gets another life at the SCG Test, 1990-91, as Boon hits the dirt.

(Photo: Gregg Porteous)

ABOVE: 'Look out, David, here it comes.' New Zealand's Dipak Patel was not impressed by Merv Hughes' short one but I've already thrown the ball skywards. Perth, first Test, 1989.
BELOW: Bowled Courtney Walsh, Trinidad, West Indies, 1991.
(Photo: Gregg Porteous)

Ignoring Desmond Haynes' request to check for the mote in his eye,
Barbados, West Indies, 1991.

(Photo: Gregg Porteous)

ABOVE: Geoff Marsh, David Boon, Mark Taylor—the 'engine room', West Indies, 1991.

(Photo: Gregg Porteous)

BELOW: I like to sing in Barbados. Victory celebrations after winning the one-day series in West Indies, 1991.

(Photo: Gregg Porteous)

ABOVE: Off to training in Antigua, West Indies, 1991 (or the Partridge Family takes up cricket?)

(Photo: Gregg Porteous)

BELOW: Australian cricket's answer to the Hells Angels, in Bermuda after the tour is over, 1991.

(Photo: Gregg Porteous)

ABOVE LEFT AND RIGHT: A Danny Morrison ball and a pull shot resulted in a broken bat and four runs in a one-day game against New Zealand, Adelaide 1989-90.

(Photo: Gregg Porteous)

BELOW: The one-dayers in Perth bring out the most inventive banners.

(Photo: Gregg Porteous)

ABOVE: The result of an accidental shirt-front with the New Zealand wicket-keeper during a one-day game at the MCG, 1990-91. I received two weeks' suspension from the dressing-room tribunal...
BELOW: India's Srikanth takes a tumble while trying to field, third Test, Sydney, 1991-92.

ABOVE: Just to show a bit of flexibility, verses India, World Cup game, Bellerive, Tasmania, 1991-92.
BELOW: Not an argument about who had the strongest thighs, rather checking Mark Taylor's jaw after he had been hit by a bouncer in the Adelaide Test against India, 1991-92.

to Simpson's comments that poor West Indian over rates had made it hard for the Australian batsmen to develop a rhythm in the middle.

'You can quote me as saying he is a moaner and bad loser,' Richards told the post-match media conference. 'It's a matter of what has happened in this series and our encounters with him, notably in Australia. The Bobby Simpsons . . . have been shouting their mouths off. I'm never in the business of shouting my mouth off about what we're going to do. Every now and then he says "thank you" or "well played" or whatever the case, but you treat people the same way how you are treated. I'm going to tell you again that Bobby Simpson ain't our cup of tea.'

Whatever the provocation, I thought Richards' outburst was unwarranted. Why say that publicly when you've won a Test series 2–0, with one match still to be played?

Australia went into that final match trying to be very positive, understandably with a lot of incentive after Richards' statement. Former West Indian paceman Andy Roberts was the curator in '91 and he provided the quickest, bounciest wicket we saw on that tour. History shows that Australia won the final Test, salvaging at least some pride from what became an extremely disappointing tour.'

JEFF DUJON

'When I first began playing Test cricket, Jeff Dujon was already a cricket legend – which was somewhat surprising, given the number of matches he had played. But Dujon seemed to emerge and star in the same movement, the wicketkeeper of the powerful West Indian team under captain Clive Lloyd.

Part of Dujon's secret, I believe, is his style. He was never a workmanlike 'keeper, in the manner of Australian gloveman Ian

Healy, who spends hours and hours practising and exercising to hone his skills. Dujon is a more laid-back character, which is reflected in his 'keeping – athletic, natural.

The wicketkeeping purist would probably challenge Dujon's footwork as demonstrating imperfect technique, but he always had that West Indian flair, the seemingly lazy gymnastic flair that made the outrageous appear easy. Of course, Dujon's technique standing up behind the stumps was also less than perfect, caused by the fact that he kept for season after season to four pacemen. However, the catches he took standing back!

I can attest, having replaced an injured Healy during World Cup matches in the '91–'92 season, that standing back to international pacemen makes the hands go numb. Stopping the ball is one thing, catching an edge another, especially when bowlers of the calibre of Malcolm Marshall and Curtly Ambrose are charging in.

The first time I met Jeff, I liked him, and at every opportunity after a game, whether it was a Test, one-dayer or team function, we would get together for a drink and a chat. I respect him as cricketer as much for his batting as his wicketkeeping. Time and time again in my Test career, Australia would be on the edge of either winning or setting up victory and Dujon would waltz in at seven or eight and make a century. In the last series in the West Indies, when many experts were questioning his place in the team because he hadn't made a 50 for some time – Dujon walked out in the first innings and made 60-odd. He played even better in the Test match in Trinidad, when the West Indies could have lost in three days if the game hadn't been rained out.

In the very first game I played for Australia, a one-dayer in 1983–84 at the MCG in Melbourne, we had the West Indies three or four wickets down for nothing. Dujon and Gus Logie got together and West Indies won the game.

In all the time I've played against the West Indies – three Test series and multiple one-day championships – I've never seen Jeff lose his temper. He's just a regular guy, who will do anything to help you out. In the West Indies in 1990, I broke a couple of bats and Dujon gave me one, which he didn't have to – it was a good 'un too. Unfortunately, he wanted it back!

Dujon has always been one to see the lighter side of cricket, which is perhaps more easily understandable because through most of his career, the West Indies have won handsomely. For example, in a Test match in Melbourne in 1988–89, I was facing Patrick Patterson on an up-and-down MCG wicket. Patrick was fired up and bowling really quickly, making survival the first consideration before scoring runs. During a scheduled interval, I walked in gratefully for the rest and refreshment to find Dujon laughing that infuriating West Indies' giggle, obviously at my expense.

'What's so funny,' I barked. 'It can't have been that funny!'

'Boon,' he said, 'today I saw one of the funniest things I have ever seen in cricket. Patrick bowled one at you and in the next second, there was not one part of your body between the ground and the stumps – you were above the stumps!'

'I suppose you would have hooked it?!' was my attempt at a caustic reply, but Dujon just kept giggling.

He is now officially retired, as much for the West Indies' recent policy of promoting younger players, which is their Board's right. However, I believe Dujon should have been given the option – because of his record and the way he played out his heart and soul for the West Indies – to announce his retirement, rather than being dropped, as was the case.'

JAMAICA

'When the Australian team arrived in Kingston, Jamaica, in 1991, we already knew that there were certain downtown areas where it was unwise for tourists, or naive cricketers, to frequent.

We were staying in the Hotel Pegasus, close to Sabina

Park – Kingston's cricket oval – but also in the near vicinity of the city jail. Whenever the Australian players went on a training run, they usually ended up leaving or returning to the Pegasus past the jail, which housed an average of 250 inmates on death row awaiting execution. I think most of those guys used to hang out the windows and abuse us. Mind you, they were there behind barbed wire and more than 50 metres from the road, but they were an extremely threatening bunch of gentlemen.

The Australians were also told never to go out alone, especially at night. That was enough for a home-town lad from Launceston – I left the hotel about three times in the 14 days we stayed there, and only in the company of half a dozen burly team-mates.

ABC cricket commentator Neville Oliver, however, is made of stronger stuff. He decided he wanted to view the Kingston night-life first-hand, so our mutual friend and former Tasmanian import Michael Holding organised a buddy to accompany Neville. Unfortunately, Big Red reported later that he called the night off fairly early. He and his 'minder' would go into this or that establishment and within a few seconds the tension of the place would rise because of the presence of a white man. However, Neville's minder would only have to say, 'It's okay, he's a mate of Michael Holding's', and the locals would calm down again.

The veteran Melbourne journalist, Tom Prior, experienced the down-side of Kingston. On tour to write a book about the West Indies, cricket, and everything, as well as visit his daughter, who lived in St Vincent, Prior hired a car and went downtown in Kingston on his own to take photographs and some notes. Unfortunately for him, he got into a situation where guns and knives were produced. Prior had to be rescued and escorted back to his hotel by the police.

At Sabina Park, the crowd was fairly even-handed – the spectators didn't mind if Australia bounced the West Indies or vice versa – just so long as someone got hit! In the first Test, both myself and Gus Logie were struck while batting. Logie was hurt quite badly and had to go off, but the crowd seemed to enjoy that even more. When he returned, the crowd went crazier.

I collected one on the chin, but being somewhat obstinate, decided not to come off for the necessary stitches. Australia's physiotherapist Errol Alcott came out to treat me, and after some rudimentary patchwork, I sent him back to the pavilion. It was after play that a local doctor stitched me up. He wanted to give me an anaesthetic, but I wouldn't let him. I don't think he could believe it and kept telling the various spectators hanging around outside the rooms all about it.'

CURTLY AMBROSE

'As a batsman, when I watch Curtly bowl, I am reminded of his predecessor, Joel Garner, because of their twin abilities to bowl an accurate line and length with unpredictable bounce.

He is also one of most inscrutable cricketers I've ever played against. Occasionally, he'll smile at you if he's sent down a good delivery, or more likely two or three in the one over – not that it's a shark's grin, more that both you and he know you were lucky to be still batting.

That first Test match of the '88–89 series, in Brisbane, was an extremely torrid one for the Australian batsmen. The night before at the team discussion, Swamp had opened up for one of his terse but stirring speeches: 'We know we're going to get hit, but when we do, we can't let them know that we're hurt. We've got to tough it out!' The next day, I opened with Geoff Marsh to Curtly pounding in, bowling at the body, Gus Logie less than a metre away at bat-pad and Roger Harper was around the corner at leg-slip. It was either duck if you could, get caught if you nicked one or get hit.

With Swamp's speech in mind and having to regularly shoulder arms as the ball whistled past my left ear, I copped one high on the ribcage under the left armpit. Luckily, the ball didn't drive me back onto my stumps, but it did knock all the air out of my lungs. I stood there with stars in my eyes, trying to remember Marsh's words.

Looking up, I saw Swamp walking down the wicket, doing a bit of gardening with his bat and wearing a wry smile.

'What?!' I hissed between clenched teeth.

'It's all right, Boonie,' answered my trusty companion, 'you can give it a rub.'

However, in the same one-dayer that I hit Malcolm Marshall for six in Sydney, Geoff Marsh and I 'nailed' Curtly. Previously, Ambrose largely forced batsmen to play shots that weren't there, because of his accuracy. But he hated getting hit for runs at any time, and if the ball went to the boundary, he rolled his eyes as if to say, 'Well, that was a lucky shot!' But that one night in Sydney, Curtly lost the plot completely. Swamp and I kept turning him over for singles, the best way to infuriate any bowler. The big fellow got extremely upset, cursing himself, us and the gods of cricket in general, forsaking his outward, laid-back image.

Curtly has also proved that he can learn from adversity. Since that one-day match, whenever he gets hit for four, he snarls at himself and reverts to line and length bowling.

Away from cricket, Ambrose is a very quiet man who loves his music, often playing a seemingly ever-present guitar.

Curtly was lured to cricket after being a promising basketballer, but Jeff Dujon once told me that Ambrose has even contemplated going back to the sport of hoops.

When he's batting, Curtly does become fired up, particularly when someone like Stephen Waugh bounces him. Steve's logic is that if he's going to cop short ones, then the bowlers who deliver them should experience a similar thrill – and 'Tugger' bowls a fair bouncer.

But Curtly has a lot of confidence in his ability with the bat. He very rarely wears a helmet and, on the principle of the pendulum, when his long arms and long body click, the ball does go an extremely long way.

But with due respect to his batting, I regard Curtly Ambrose as perhaps one current bowler who will join the greats.'

WASIM AKRAM

'My lasting impression of Wasim Akram, the Pakistani left-arm paceman, occurred in Perth during a one-day game in 1989–90. The WACA wicket was affected by some quite severe cracks, which made Akram an immediately difficult and dangerous proposition because of his ability to swing the ball both ways. And how he swings it away from a right-hander when he's bowling around the wicket escapes me – he must be a very, very talented cricketer!

That day in Perth, I was deliberating whether to wear my preferred cap or opt for the protective helmet. As the umpires walked out onto the field, I picked up the hard-hat – a fortuitous decision, in the end.

One of Akram's predictable, but effective, tactics is to come around the wicket early on in an innings before the shine has had any time to come off the ball. He did so, and I went back to cut a shortish ball outside off-stump. Before I had time to react, the ball had smashed into the visor on the left-hand side of the face. Head spinning, my immediate thought was: 'You wouldn't be too sharp if you'd worn the cap, son!' So I changed the visor, shook my head, and kept batting.

Akram is perhaps the best bowler in the world at tail-cleaning, the paceman's treasured art of bowling the last the batsmen – Nine, Ten, Jack – to end an innings. In the Sharjah tournament in 1989, Akram dismissed Craig McDermott, Terry Alderman and Carl Rackemann with three balls – 3–0. Alderman and Rackemann are recognised as

bunnies, albeit experienced non-batters, but McDermott is a fair batsman. Akram just sped in with that lightning-fast, 10-pace run-up, from
around the wicket, and bowled three, huge, in-swinging yorkers.

When Australia toured England in 1989, I had a chat with Akram
during the game against Lancashire, because he was out injured.
He's a quiet young man, who always says hello off the pitch, unlike
some. On-field, he has a lot of aggression, like most fast bowlers.'

ALLAN LAMB

'Allan Lamb is another cricketer whom I would class as a friend
rather than a friendly opponent. Certainly, Lamb's record is somewhat
surprising, because he hasn't enjoyed as much success as one would
expect outside England. However, his record against the West Indies
in unbelievable. At one stage, 'Leg-o' had eight Test centuries, six
against the lads from the Caribbean.

Lamb enjoys life and he enjoys cricket. He and his wife Lindsay
have always extended an invitation of hospitality to the Boon family
in England, which has become a reciprocal arrangement in Australia.

When Australia toured England in 1989, Allan Border, Geoff Marsh
and I were asked by Lamb to come to his home in Northamptonshire
for a traditional South African barbeque – a braaivleis. When we
arrived, we were greeted by Lamb, Lindsay and Lamb's sister. Lindsay
asked me where Pip was – which opened a can of worms about
the Australian touring party not travelling with wives.

I had argued in the Australian team meetings before the tour
began that wives and partners should be allowed to accompany
the players. However, the decision went the other way and I stood
by the team policy. However, that one simple question turned into
an enormous debate between Lindsay, AB and Lamb's sister – the
Australian captain under the hammer from both sides.

Basically, the girls argued, Border was a male chauvinistic pig, which didn't overly thrill the skipper. As the party progressed it was revealed that Lamb's sister was a good golfer and she issued a challenge to Border that she would play off the men's tees and thrash him. Somewhere in among the ruckus, Lamb, Marsh and Boon escaped the battle-scene and perched ourselves in front of a television to watch the golf.

Lamb is respected world-wide for his cricket ability, although he has struggled of late with injuries, most noticeably with a nagging hamstring strain in the World Cup in Australia.

During that tournament, Lamb was to be found with Ian Botham, both of whom were often tailed by Laurie Brown, the English physiotherapist. Brown was understandably interested in Lamb's swift recovery from his leg injury. Leg-o was indeed concentrating on rehabilitation and relaxation. 'I am looking after myself,' Lamb said to Brown one night, 'I'm only drinking two bottles a day instead of six!'

Lamb is one of those characters who, upon seeing an opponent struck in the groin region, is the first to loom overhead laughing. But, he's also the first one in to your dressing room for a chat – whether he's got a duck or 100.

The practice of opposing teams socialising after the day's play sadly is dwindling in modern cricket. I know that as captain of Tasmania, which boasts one of the youngest and least experienced teams in the Sheffield Shield, if we had the opportunity to play a touring English party, I would want players of Lamb's ilk to spend time with my players.'

IAN BOTHAM

'Books, Hollywood ventures, his own clothing label – nothing daunts Ian 'Beefy' Botham. However, neither is Botham's nature explained.

The man thrives on challenge, especially against Australia, as he has shown on so many occasions. Like Allan Lamb, Botham enjoys life, a laugh and playing up to the media. He reminds me more of Dean Jones than anyone in Australia – just like Deano, Botham isn't afraid to try anything, and whether he's batting, bowling or fielding, he gives everything. Plus, they both have extremely extrovert personalities and ooze sporting talent.

Botham is renowned as a hitter of the ball, but it's because his technique is very, very good that he has had so much success – and why he can play effectively as an opener. Botham's original philosophy with his bowling was sheer aggression, but as time and age have slowed him, so his pace has mellowed. But the rat-cunning and cricket brain haven't disappeared.

One of my strongest memories of the Botham nous came on the Australian tour of England in 1985 at Old Trafford. Botham was bowling to Wayne Phillips, who was a wicked cutter of the cricket ball. One theory, which permeates all sport, is to exploit the opposition's weakness; Botham that day showed how your opponent's strength can be used to your advantage.

He set two slips, two gullies, a forward point and a backward point – and he bowled short and outside off-stump. Five times the ball smashed into the pickets. On the sixth ball 'Flipper' was caught in the gully. Botham had dared Phillips to wield one of his potent weapons – 1–20 was the result.

I was also watching Mr Botham in England in 1981 – I was there playing League cricket with Netherfield – when he demolished Australia in the legendary Headingley Test.

In 1986–87, I witnessed his century in Brisbane, especially his personal bout with Merv Hughes – the quicker the big Victorian bowled them, the further Botham hit them. I was fielding at mid-off and Merv pleaded: 'What am I going to do?' 'Try line and length,' was my reply. Hughes tried to bounce Botham and got hit out of the park; the one pitched up was hit back over his head for four – 'Good philosophy, Boonie,' snarled Merv, although his notion of line and length and mine didn't quite match.

I remember Victorian medium-pacer Simon Davis bowling to

Botham in a one-dayer in Perth and the big Englishman smashed him for 26 in one over. Allan Border set a deep mid-on and deep mid-off, only two metres off the sightscreen. Botham was hitting Davis so hard and straight, the outfielders couldn't cut the ball off!

Many people, cricket experts and fans, love to hate Botham because of the sometimes outrageous way he plays cricket and similar behaviour that has often been highlighted in the media. But I have always regarded Botham as one of cricket's greatest challenges, for the very reason that he will try anything to either dismiss you or score runs.

In that 1986–87 Test in Brisbane, Bruce Reid was last man out for Australia at 5.49 pm and we had to follow-on. Geoff Marsh and I were despatched to face one over, but instead of Graham Dilley or Phil DeFreitas, the ball was thrown to Botham – of course!

It was Swampy's turn to take first ball so I was feeling slightly better about the situation. First ball: Marsh, single to fine leg. Second: Boon, single to fine leg. Third: Marsh, single to fine leg. There followed three balls from Botham in extra-weird mode – side-winding to the wicket, a two-step run-up and one with his arms and legs flailing! Only he would try this approach in a Test match; only he would dare.

With the exception of the World Cup in 1987, Botham has played in every Test and one-day series against Australia since I started playing for my country. In 1989, at Old Trafford, Botham will be remembered for playing an horrendous shot and getting out to leg-spinner Trevor Hohns. Beefy was trying to hit 'Cracker' into the railway station – if he'd succeeded, Botham would have been a hero. He missed. But the legend of Ian Botham lives on, not over yet, stronger than ever.'

JOHN EMBUREY

'On Australia's tour of England in 1985 and when the English came out to Australia the next summer, I was John Emburey's regular victim.

But it was the great English off-spinner who was one player who improved my batting technique immeasurably. In those two seasons of cricket, Emburey either dismissed me himself or tied me up so much that if I got to the other end, I got myself out through frustration.

But in the winter of 1987, I worked harder than ever before to improve my play against spin bowling. The result? The Bicentennial Test in Sydney, when I played much more positively to finish 184 not out. To come out on top of 'Embers' after two seasons of sheer misery was very satisfying.

The main technical aspects I worked on to combat Emburey were using my feet and trying to judge the flight of the ball – that way you can decide whether to attack or play back and work the ball.

Because of Emburey's action, a batsman had to play positively and go down the wicket. But because he could hold the ball back in his hand, he could change the direction and style of delivery, leaving you stranded in no-man's land.

I had been playing one way and not scoring runs; if you're not scoring, you're going to get out, because you can't rotate the strike. To 'beat' a spinner, you have force him off his preferred line and length, make him change his favoured bowling style. You do that by improving your footwork and your ability to judge the length of any given delivery.

Having found my confidence against spinners, I feel extremely positive whenever Australia plays in Sydney – the old phobia about an SCG turner (a dying breed of wicket, anyway) just doesn't phase me. But the Sydney wicket does turn and if you don't bowl well there, you will get hammered.

I like to think that Australia plays the SCG like New South Wales plays there in the Sheffield Shield – the Bluebaggers just own the ground. The New South Wales players exude an air that says, 'We're going to beat you!' The other States believe fervently that the Sydney wicket will turn at right angles and therefore a draw is the optimal result. Me? I just think it's a great place to play cricket, because of its history, the grandstands and the skyline around the oval.

The last time I duelled with Emburey was on the 1989 tour of England, when Australia played Middlesex in a three-day game at Lord's. I was batting with Allan Border and had gone down the wicket and hit Embers through extra cover a couple of times. This had understandably annoyed him, and watching me come down the wicket again, Emburey held the ball back and I was left half-stranded. But I blasted away, full-length into my follow-through – the ball landed on the top of the Long Room. Emburey turned to AB and said: 'I thought I'd done him then!'

He was an exceptional off-spinner and a good bloke – he had to be, he married an Australian!'

DAVID GOWER

'The majority of international cricketers were born with cricket ability but have had to work hard – some incredibly so – to achieve their position. But some athletes have the Gift, the natural skills to just walk out and play the game. David Gower is one such person.

Unfortunately, at least for David, modern cricket, like other sports, adopted strict training regimes at all levels. Gower was dropped from the England Test team at the start of 1991, his skipper Graham Gooch stating that the elegant left-hander didn't fit the necessary mould. He was recalled for Pakistan's recent tour to England but again, sadly, was omitted from the England squad that went to India in 1993. His experience would have been greatly valued there.

Understandably, it's hard to argue with Gower's Test record, however one might assess his attitude. As an opponent, you know that Gower will almost always give you a chance early in his innings, especially in the gully area. However, the opportunity won't be easy, because he hits the ball so sweetly – it's always hummin'.

Gower's desire to play and succeed for England is masked by his laid-back nature, which works against him when he has a run of bad luck. While he stays laid-back, his critics carp that he doesn't work hard enough.

I will never forget Gower's 1985 series against Australia in England – 166 in the third Test at Trent Bridge, 215 in the fifth Test at Edgbaston and 157 at the Oval in the sixth and final match of the series. I also clearly remember that Australia's 1989 tour, when we whitewashed England 4-0, was somewhat disastrous for Gower. Australian captain Allan Border knew exactly how Gower felt, having been defeated 3-1 in 1985.

In '85, Gower invited all the Australian players – as well as his own team-mates – to have dinner at his home in Leicester. On tour, the visiting players usually become bored with hotel or restaurant fare and the chance to relax away from the public eye is very much appreciated.

Geoff Marsh did the same for the Australians and the Indians last summer during the last Test in Perth – even though 'Swampy' wasn't playing. The Indians had never experienced or heard of such a custom, but welcomed the opportunity to socialise with their opponents on a different level from any other time on tour.

Gower has been a rebel, a captain who stood up for his players, and is known for his anti-administration stance. One humorous story about Gower's attitude relates to his practice of wearing coloured socks on the playing field, as opposed to traditional creams or greys. At one stage, Gower wore red socks in the field and blue socks in which to bat!

Legend has it that Lord Ted Dexter, the TCCB chairman, approached Gower one day in the England dressing room and asked:

'What colour socks are those?' Gower replied: 'Can't you see, Mr Chairman, they are blue!'

David Gower has done a lot for the game of cricket through the pleasure he has given to countless fans. But he is a man whose manner leaves him open to easy criticism.'

STEPHEN AND MARK WAUGH

'In my first year as captain of Tasmania, Mark Taylor and Mark Waugh opened for New South Wales at the TCA Ground in Hobart. Taylor has often chided Mark that he has taken the easy way out, becoming an all-rounder like his twin Stephen, rather than staying in the 'engine room'.

I have, of course, known Stephen for longer than Mark, because the latter took longer to break onto the Australian scene. But my gut reaction about such questions is that Australian cricket is extremely lucky to have two brothers, let alone twins, who are so talented.

The pair of them fit into the category of 'naturals', although they both work extremely hard on their games. Visibly, the Waughs do things easier and better than most other people. Okay, they chose cricket as their main sport, but put either Steve or Mark behind a golf ball and it's gone – out of sight!

What makes them particularly special is their indifference, in the best way, to their innate abilities. They appreciate it – the gift to pick up a tennis racquet or table tennis bat and play as though born with it grafted to the hand – but just don't get carried away.

Knowing both of them, I would say that Mark is probably the more confident of the two. Perhaps it stemmed from his waiting in wings longer – maybe he's just a cheeky beggar!

On debut against England in Adelaide, Mark scored a century. Re-entering the dressing-room, after the crowd and his team-mates had risen as one to applaud a superb knock, Mark commented: 'I don't know why you guys said Test cricket was so hard!'

You know it's tongue in cheek, but the things he gets away with! He once told Allan Border, Australia's most prolific run-scorer, that AB wouldn't have made it at Test level if the better cricketers hadn't been playing in the original World Series! Allan just laughed. I'm still shaking my head at Mark's audacity.

The Waughs, they bat, bowl, field like jets, and are blessed with very good hands. As twins, they don't appear to be very close at all – the operative word being 'appear'. Maybe they don't seem to socialise, or talk together as brothers are supposed to, but who's to know how twins are to behave in international cricket? As they have both said, they enjoy each other's success and want to see each other do well. It's also worth noting that Stephen and Mark are vying for the same spot in the Australian team as middle-order batsmen and medium-pace bowlers.

In the West Indies in 1990, Mark copped a barrage through the series, especially in the first Test in Jamaica. However, the day Mark scored a century in the first innings in Antigua was a special innings to witness. Towards its end, Mark was so confident, he was backing away from Curtly Ambrose and cutting him for six over backward point. In the laid-back parlance of the game, that's 'good shooting'.

Stephen has had his ups and downs, but England '89 was special, when he scored 506 runs at 125.50. In his early days, the younger Stephen was called on to do so much for his country, earning the tag of 'Iceman' for his one-day bowling. In the 1987 World Cup, it was Stephen who was called upon to bowl at the 'death' overs, the final four to six overs when batsmen will do absolutely anything to score runs. Steve just showed maturity beyond his years and accepted every challenge and won most.

I believe that if Stephen and Mark are both playing well, there is room in the Australian Test team for both of them. What is staggering is to think that they are only 26 years old and Stephen has already played over 40 Test matches and more than 120 one-day games. As their respective records stand, Stephen has bowled more for Australia than Mark, but they are both very aggressive, willing to try anything to take a wicket.

Mark was once dubbed 'Junior' or even 'Afghanistan' (for the Forgotten War), but his latest tag is 'Golden Bollocks'. Time and time again, when nothing is happening on a Test ground, AB will toss the ball to Mark – result: wicket. Hence the nickname.

Before Stephen first hurt his back, he was quite a quick bowler for a medium pacer. But that injury caused his batting to fall away and he has found, as anyone would, that it's very hard to break back into the Australian team if you give 'a sucker an even break'.

That 'sucker' was, of course, Mark. When Mark was selected, Stephen was very disappointed, but he would have been whoever had taken his place. I spent a lot of time with Stephen in England in 1989. Pip and his wife-to-be Lynette travelled together in the United Kingdom. Pip was Lynette's matron of honour at her marriage to Stephen in 1991 and our daughter Georgina was their flower girl.

Stephen has a very dry wit, coupled with a vivid imagination that has a wicked edge when it comes to practical jokes.

Mark, like me, played a lot of Sheffield Shield cricket before he was selected for Australia. I made my Shield debut in 1978–79, played my first one-day game for Australia in 1984 and won a Test cap in 1984–85 in Brisbane. Mark first played Shield in 1984–85 and played his first Test against England in Adelaide in 1990–91.

Stephen and Mark, along with Mark Taylor, represent the younger brigade of New South Wales, a state which has long been strong in the Shield competition. All three are very good players, who came to Test cricket far more confident than, for example, I did.

IAN HEALY

'Ian Healy is one of the fashion gurus of the Australian cricket team. Put that down to working in the fashion business with his father-in-law – or perhaps the wicketkeeper's traditional trait of close attention to detail. Healy is forever cleaning his kit, making sure his wicketkeeping gloves are just right, hand-massaged, ready for that one nick – understandably, given the importance of his position. Before Healy emerges into the daylight, every article of external clothing has been ironed, every hair is in place.

Healy's rise to the role of Australian wicketkeeper has been well-documented. He was Queensland's second gloveman, but when the incumbent Peter Anderson was injured, Healy moved up into the Maroon line-up. Healy actually replaced Greg Dyer, the New South Welsh 'keeper who copped all the flak for admitting that he wasn't one hundred per cent sure about a leg-side catch in a Test match against New Zealand in Melbourne in 1987–88. In fact, so few Sheffield Shield matches had Healy played before his selection, that his Test appearances soon easily outstripped his first-class record.

The one dominant factor in Healy's cricket life is an amazing aptitude for sheer, hard work. If he doesn't catch 1000 balls a day during the cricket season, I'm sure he suffers withdrawal symptoms. If he's not catching the ball at practice, it's before or after breakfast in the hotel carpark, ricocheting a golf ball off various walls and angles, honing his reflexes, his hand-eye co-ordination, his fitness.

And Healy is fit. If Dean Jones is rated the quickest between wickets, perhaps the fastest in the world, and Craig McDermott has a physique and stamina trained to Iron-Man levels, Healy is up there with both.

The general public, let alone some cricketers, never fully realise the amount of agility, strength and endurance a wicketkeeper at Test or one-day level must achieve. I do. I found out filling in for Healy in two World Cup games at the end of the 1991–92 summer.

I rate him as good as any wicketkeeper in the world, basically because he has worked so hard to attain his present level. Ian may not be as athletic as, for example, a Jeff Dujon, but he still takes some spectacular catches. He is very technique conscious and possesses very good footwork and over several years at international level, Healy's overall improvement has been extremely impressive.

Healy's nickname is Savlon, as in 'Savlon Heals', the advertising campaign for the antiseptic cream, which gets shortened to 'Sav'. However, the sarcasm which is often inherent in such tags could have been far worse after Healy's first Test match against Pakistan in Karachi in 1988.

Australian legend Rod Marsh wore 'Iron Gloves' when he first made the team but Healy's could have been similar – or worse – after dropping three or four catches. Unfortunately for young Ian, the ones he put down weren't difficult, just the agonising sort for wicketkeeper, bowler and surrounding fieldsmen – straight in and out. But Healy's hard work has paid off to such an extent that now he makes 'keeping look easy.

Left-arm paceman Bruce Reid is an especially difficult bowler to 'keep to because of his height and the way he makes the ball bounce awkwardly. When Ian was behind the stumps to 'Chook' Reid in a one-dayer, revered commentator Richie Benaud pointed out that Healy made taking the ball look easy because of his correct technique.

Healy is an aggressive cricketer, a man who backs himself behind the stumps or with the bat in his hand against the best in the world. His batting has improved to the point where he is now regarded as a major contributor to the innings, where his failure to score runs now earns more comment than his success. And his ability to judge a run, coupled with his speed, makes him an attacking one-day batsman.

Healy's other big attribute is his heart, his desire to play for his country. When Ian tore his hamstring during the 1992 World Cup,

Australian captain Allan Border finally had to order him not to play, so that the muscle could mend. I ended up spending a lot of time with 'Heal', as he tried to make me into a makeshift gloveman.

Eventually, after missing two games, he came back – probably before he really should have done, strapped up like a racehorse. But he just kept putting in, ignoring the obvious discomfort, let alone pain, and looking for sympathy from no one.'

BRUCE REID

'No one questions Bruce Reid's ability as a fast bowler. He has height, pace and the ability to bounce the ball awkwardly for any batsman – left- or right-hander. However, his recurring back injuries have made his very selection a possible liability because of the chance he might break down.

I fear that when Bruce Reid stops playing cricket, some will ask the question, 'What if?' for his unfulfilled talent. But Reid will not be condemned for his affliction, because few people have worked so hard or endured so much to play their chosen sport.

One can view the Sheffield Shield competition over any given decade and probably tick the names of a dozen or more players who had the talent to play for Australia, but just 'didn't go on with it'. Reid has done it all – at Test and one-day level. But he is restricted by a steel plate which lies in the bottom of his spine, literally fusing his back together, the result of three operations to repair major damage.

Reid has been my friend throughout our Australian careers. He suffered a major 'downer' in West Indies in 1991, coming off an excellent season against England the summer before, when he suffered further back problems. Understandably, when Reid feels a twinge anywhere, he fears the worst. This time it was a muscle spasm, nothing severe, but enough to keep him out of the first Test side in Jamaica.

When I roomed with him in the West Indies, 'Chook' was definitely moody, but that was to be expected, given the run he was having.

Reid worked hard when he came home to Australia, but in Sydney before the third Test match against India, he broke down again. Australia had to go into that match with only two pacemen – Craig McDermott and Merv Hughes – and came very close to losing.

The experts say that a good test of a paceman is his ability to take wickets on the sub-continent, in India or Pakistan. Reid went to Pakistan in 1988 and returned home with 14 wickets from three Test matches.

It is sobering to think that Reid has missed more than three years' cricket through operations, recovery and further injury. You can have nothing but admiration for his ability to keep fighting back, hampered by something that is simply beyond his control. He admitted to me once that, after the final surgery to repair his back, he was reduced to tears with the post-operative pain. Reid wondered whether he would be able to face that level of agony again after such a shattering experience. But he keeps coming back for more.

People look at Reid and say, 'He'd be all right if he put on some weight.' One winter, Bruce went on a weight program – in fact, his build doesn't do justice to his strength – but he didn't gain an ounce. If I'd done the same program, I'd have blown up with muscle and been unable to move. The next winter, Reid decided to eat and drink as much as he could to put on weight. We're talking two and three steaks at a sitting, hamburgers, milkshakes, bananas – everything! Same result: Reid's weight remained unchanged.

Personally, this was extremely upsetting. I can't look at a pie or a hamburger without kilograms appearing out of thin air around my midriff!

But one thing is certain. If Reid is fit, he is always among the first players selected for Australia.'

ALLAN BORDER

'How do I describe the man who has been my captain for all but one, my first, of the Test matches I have ever played? He is my good friend; he possesses a strong character and a great love for his country and commitment to his team – Australia.

Border has played more Test matches than anyone else in Australian cricket history. It is perhaps the merest insight into Allan Border's character and depth of feeling for his country and friends that I have actually been 'captain' of Australia for about three days in total because of his disappointment about different situations.

My first time as stand-in skipper came in 1986 in New Zealand, when Australia had lost a one-day match in Dunedin – following hard on the heels of a defeat in Christchurch. Border was extremely angry at our performance, which is the captain's prerogative. After the match, Australia's manager Bob Merriman came to me and said that AB wasn't going to speak to the media. Merriman said that he wanted me to do the honours – to this day I don't know why he didn't ask Ray Bright, who was the vice-captain. So in I went to the media conference. It was bit horrific, but I came out of it all right.

I found AB and asked him why he didn't want to talk to the gentlemen of the Fourth Estate – he replied that he wanted to think about the day's play and didn't want to keep the journalists waiting.

The second time I was stand-in skipper came in the summer of 1991–92, when Geoff Marsh and Mark Waugh were dropped for the last Test against India in Perth. The Australian team was announced at the end of the fourth Test in Adelaide. AB did not agree with the decision to axe Marsh and Waugh.

You could never question Allan's commitment and support for the players in whom he believed. 'Swampy' was his right-hand man, the person who had backed him up as Australian cricket dragged itself out of the mire and went onto World Cup success in 1987, the Ashes 4–0 sweep in 1989 and consistent Test and one-day victories at home and abroad. Mark Waugh was an up-and-coming cricketer, regarded as one of the best in the world, who scored a century on debut and had proved himself on the tour of the West Indies. As a player, it gives you a lot of confidence to know that your captain is right behind you. But when the Australian team flew out, Allan remained behind, as he admitted later, a very disappointed man. So, I got to 'captain' Australia for almost two days.

The boys loved me! Usually, Australia begins the Perth Test with a long net session on the first morning we arrive. But because we'd just played a hard match, coach Bob Simpson called off fielding training. The lads all thought I had input into Simmo's decision, so much so they wanted to make me permanent skipper! But then AB turned up and I was again deposed.

The first time I can remember playing against Allan Border was when he wore New South Wales' colours – he made a century against Tasmania in Sydney. Since that time, we've built a strong relationship and friendship, based on mutual respect. When Border first accepted the captaincy, Australia wasn't consistent at Test level – in fact, we lost matches regularly.

On that 1986 tour of New Zealand, Border publicly threatened to resign – only because he cared so much for Australian cricket and wanted to jar the whole team into improving its performance. At the time, his Test-match total eclipsed that of the rest of the entire touring party. Stephen Waugh and David Gilbert were new caps and Geoff Marsh has only just started playing for Australia. Apart from Greg Ritchie, Wayne Phillips and myself, Border felt – probably correctly – that he didn't really have many long-term friends in his own team.

Unknowingly, but understandably, many of the players had put Allan – the last player of the mighty era of the 1970s – on a pedestal, which is not Border's way. However, the situation (like most in life) was double-sided. Border's daily routine involved playing cricket, back to the hotel, meal, few beers and bed, ready for the

next day. The younger players were interested in life outside the
hotel, such as meals at restaurants and taking more time to wind
down after a day's play.

But their major obstacle was that they felt they couldn't approach
Border to fully discuss their own problems. In my capacity as a
reasonably senior player, I told my team-mates that 'the man isn't
God', no matter how good a cricketer he might be. I said that Allan
Border was still a member of the Australian team – he couldn't
just be expected to make runs time and time again like a machine
(although he made a fair impression of one!).

Border needed his team-mates' support as much as the next man.
Over a period of years, as the Australian team became a more
cohesive unit, this hurdle was overcome and Border is now the
epitome of a very strong captain.

The media once nicknamed him 'Captain Crabby' – which was
a superficial appraisal of the man. He did become upset, but only
when it was justified – when we didn't perform to our capabilities.
Knowing how much Allan feels about Australian cricket, how could
he be different? He was captain of Australia, his country, and we
were not playing well and weren't winning.

Some people could have kept on laughing, looking for the positive,
but not Allan – he knew we could play better. He believed that
the situation didn't warrant excuses or excess humour. The media
would criticise the situation and his attitude, which would make
Border even more upset. But in the past four or five years, as
Australian cricket has become stronger, Border's relationship with
the media has been strengthened in accordance with that success.

I also believe that the system of having Border, media manager
Ian McDonald and coach Bob Simpson to okay or decline interviews
is worthwhile. I know that journalists on tour will canvass a line
of questioning with McDonald or Simpson before tackling any player.

One facet of Allan's captaincy that has always impressed me
is his ability to take one of his players to task without humiliating
them in front of their peers, the other Australian cricketers. When

Andrew Hilditch, who retired from first-class cricket in 1991–92, was in the depths of his compulsive hooking phase, Border kept advising him about it privately. In the end, Allan did say something in front of the team about 'Digger's' situation, but only as a last resort.

I can recall batting with Allan once in a day-night game against New Zealand in Sydney. I had made 60-odd and AB's advice was to 'keep consolidating and don't do anything silly'. One over later, I tried to put Stuart Gillespie over the members' stand and was comprehensively bowled. As I left the middle, I just caught a glimpse of the black look on Border's face. Luckily, Allan made quite a few runs himself.

As the rest of the game progressed, I sat in the dressing room, not actually filled with overwhelming trepidation, but knowing that I deserved, and was going to cop, a serve. When Allan got out and was close to the pavilion, I nudged the player alongside and said, 'Watch this.' Border came in, looked at me darkly and went to the rear of the room to take off his pads and relax. Eventually, he motioned for me to come closer. He started with, 'What the hell do you think that was?' and warmed to the topic. Eventually he calmed down and had his justifiable shot at me away from the others in the team.

I have the utmost respect for Border as a cricketer and a man. Because of our mutual respect for one another, I know that I can voice my opinions with him. One instance where I have disagreed with Allan was the issue of 'wives on tour' in England, '89. I don't believe that wives detract from players' performance on tour – when you're playing in Australia, your home environment is paramount. Cricketers are all different: some stay up late, others go to bed early. If your lifestyle affects your cricket performance, you don't play well and you get dropped from the Australian team.

But before we left for England, the rule was enforced. I abided by it and Pip abided by it – that was that. But some players, who had agreed with the 'no wives' rule at its inception, disobeyed it during our time in England and that really annoyed me. Allan Border and I are from the same school – Australian cricket is of utmost importance. Therefore, anything which helps Australian cricket is what should happen.

AB is initially a bit hard to get to know but, unknown to many people, who only see his public face, he's a bloody good bloke. He possesses strong ideals, but you always know where you stand. There is no need for me to comment on Allan's cricket ability – his run-scoring feats and character when Australia has been under pressure speak for themselves. Border not only surpassed Sir Donald Bradman's Test aggregate but is now the highest scorer of runs in Test cricket – that says it all.'

6

WATCHERS AND
PLAYERS

GEOFF MARSH ON BOON

David Boon is more than just a fine cricketer. He is a first-class fellow and one of the finest ambassadors and team players Australia has produced.

'Boonie' comes across as the quiet type. He lets his actions in the centre, irrespective of the state of the match, do his talking for him. But underneath it all, 'Babs' has plenty to say.

He is a strong motivator in team meetings and always one of the first and loudest when we break into the proud Australian team song at the end of a successful Test or important one-day international assignment. Boonie is what playing team sport is all about. He is a close friend to his team-mates and a great tourist.

We go back a long way and have become more than cricket buddies. In the Australian team, particularly through the successes of recent times, there have been plenty of great blokes. The entire team is close. But with Boonie, there is something special.

Our wives and children, despite living on opposite sides of Australia for much of the year, are extremely close.

We first met at an Australian Under-19 trial match, just prior to the announcement of the youth team to tour England in 1977. The rotund, little 16-year-old bloke from Tasmania turned up out of nowhere and peeled off a hundred!

We were both selected for that tour and soon afterwards began bumping into each other on the Sheffield Shield circuit. However, it wasn't until December 1985 that we renewed our acquaintance at international level. By the end of that Test match against India – my first – we had taken the first real steps towards what we cherish as quite a proud record together in the Australian team.

It was over a beer, in the famous Charlie's Bar at the Adelaide Hilton Hotel, that we vowed together to win the opening spots in the national team and stay there for a very long time. He was almost the perfect partner with whom to bat.

All the Aussies are good to bat with – after all, you're representing your country. But with Babs there's that something special. We had an almost unique understanding; we got to the stage where calling wasn't even necessary. Running between wickets with Boonie was almost a second instinct.

He knows me and I understand him. We also comprehend when the other is struggling. In those circumstances, the best place to recover concentration is at the other end. So a quick single helps the partnership.

Whenever we meet in the middle, after an over is completed, Boonie remains his typical quiet self – unless he's played a pearler of a shot during that over! That's when he wants to talk about life, or more to the point, the shot.

He certainly did some chirping the day we established a world record on the tour of India in 1986, the famous tied Test series. Babs and I opened the innings and rattled up just over 200 and were pretty happy with ourselves when, with 13 overs to go and 10 wickets in hands, we went to the final drinks break. The Indians soon put an end to our plans of a score in excess of 300 for the day – the interval went for 15 minutes and we were informed from the Australian dressing room that only five more overs would be bowled. Boonie had plenty to say about the Indian tactics.

Touring as much as cricketers do, playing cricket all the time and living in each other's pockets, it takes special characters to cope with the many moods and habits of different team-mates. Boonie was the perfect room-mate for me on many tours. We share so many common interests. But like the co-operation that can be so vital in the tense atmosphere of competition against fast bowlers, Boonie can read his team-mates' moods too.

After only my sixth Test, against New Zealand in Auckland, I was pretty downcast. We'd lost the Test and the series to the Kiwis in the same match that I had notched my first Test hundred. I, like Boonie and any Australian cricketer with pride, take losing pretty hard. It hurts like hell. But Boonie knew there was still something worth celebrating. He'd made two Test hundreds by this time and knew how tough it was to reach three figures in the big arena. He insisted we celebrate.

And we did. In a big way. We snuck away from the team hotel and found a local pub in the back streets of Auckland. By around 11 o'clock, we knew we'd done enough celebrating – in fact, we knew we'd had one or two too many. So we headed back to the hotel, via the local caravan hot dog and hamburger stand.

Now any hardened drinker knows just how well a greasy hamburger, with the lot, goes down after a night on the singing syrup. About a kilometre from the hotel – munching rather indelicately on the fat-riddled, sauce-laden, sobering burger in drizzly and chilly Kiwi weather – Boonie lost his footing on the edge of the slippery curb. Next thing, with the safety of those delicious burgers our number-one priority, we were both in the gutter.

It would have capped the off Test series if Richard Hadlee, Jeremy

Coney, Brendon Bracewell and the like could have seen us. Let alone Simmo – we couldn't let him know. Hamburgers intact, we continued our journey back to the hotel.

To this day, Simmo doesn't know about how the nation's two opening batsmen of the time were left lying in an Auckland gutter, giggling uncontrollably, after a series loss. If he'd seen our muddied, tomato-sauce-splattered shirts and trousers the next morning, he'd have had a fair idea.

It was Boonie's turn again to suffer from an aberration of the laughing juice early on the historic Ashes tour of England in 1989. After being labelled the worst Australian team to visit the Mother Country and facing the inglorious record of Aussie teams at Headingley, we won the Leeds Test match, the first, by a healthy 210 runs. The celebrations were just as healthy, with the blessing of the team's management, but they were followed by a bus trip to Manchester, where we were scheduled to play Lancashire the very next day.

Babs, to say the least, celebrated as hard, if not harder, than the rest of the team. There wasn't much of anything left on the top shelf of the bars on the bus or hotel the next day, thanks to Boonie and Tom Moody, who'd been twelfth man.

A simple three-day recovery in a 'friendly' with Lancashire would be just the tonic for Boonie and the boys after the Test victory. But the inclusion of fiery Pakistani fast bowler Wasim Akram and West Indies paceman Patrick Patterson cast a rather different complexion on the match. Luckily, Australia lost the toss – my call as acting-captain was just as clouded as the boys' heads after the celebration.

So we were forced into the field. That's where Boonie brought the house down. Not with one of the many blinding catches which he has pulled off at short leg throughout his distinguished Test and first-class career – but one of his biggest boo-boos.

In the game's second over, on a bright, crisp English morning, Boonie's fellow Tasmanian Greg Campbell got a hot delivery to lift on the Lancashire opener, the ball taking the top edge of his face-protecting blade. It lobbed gently towards the unsuspecting, tired-looking Aussie bat-pad specialist. Panic set in immediately. All Babs wanted was a good twelve hours' sleep and not to be responsible for ending this poor Lancastrian's innings. Boonie fumbled his way forward to at least make an attempt at completing the catch. But when a fielder fails to even make contact with the ball, the batsman is a pretty good chance to survive. He sure did.

The entire Australian team fell to the ground in fits of laughter. As acting-captain, I had to restore some form of order, or at least look as though I was perturbed at the missed chance. I proceeded to bag the boys and instruct them to get on the clash, as Boonie re-arranged his protective helmet, which had almost totally obstructed his view as he staggered and slipped to the ground, trying to avoid international embarrassment.

I decided the best place to be was in the slips cordon, from where I could take full control of the match. In the very next over – as Mike Veletta at second slip and Steve Waugh at third continued to giggle at Boonie's demise – a speedy Geoff Lawson delivery was edged straight into my midriff region. In and out!

The second catch in two overs had gone to turf and this time it was the skipper's fault. By the end of the day, the Aussie tourists had grassed an incredible nine catches. And we still cleaned up Lancashire for 179!

Boonie's day ended in classic, forgettable fashion. He waddled out to bat at number three, after Veletta had gone for a duck. But Boonie's eyesight hadn't improved; he was clean bowled by big Patrick for a golden duck. I don't think he saw that ball either.

There wasn't much to be said at the close of play that night. Certainly, no one felt like a beer to soak up the day's proceedings. But everyone slept soundly.

Boonie's other great attribute is knowing when to say or do the right thing, especially in the communal existence of hotel and motel living. We'd often go for long walks together, in between our regular training and playing commitments. He's good for a chat and a beer as light relief from the pressure of the game.

Being a farmer at heart, I like to get back to my roots when away from home. Boonie understood that desire, but it often embarrassed him on the morning of a big match, when we'd go through our regular ritual of breakfast together – after I'd wake him up – and our long walk to get the mind focused on the big task ahead: opening for our country.

We'd often walk long distances and spend an hour or two away from the hotel, especially on the days when Australia played day-night games, which don't kick off until after lunch. I always wanted to find the R.M. Williams shops, which specialise in articles of farm clothing and attire. Boonie, unfortunately, is a bit of yuppie at heart. A fashion expert of the Pierre Cardin, Country Road and Jag set. It embarrassed the little Tasmanian to spend time in my company, admiring the latest farm dress boots, which keep the feet warm on those frosty mornings shearing sheep or driving the seed tractors. But he put up with it, because it was part of our successful routine. It created some good humour, too.

Like a good friend, Boonie has put up with a lot. But that's the sort of guy that he is. He's a fair dinkum Aussie. One of the best.

PIP BOON

To the enquiring public eye, a cricketer's life is male-dominated. Whether it be through the Australian domestic summer or on international tours, the national team is almost a separate, hallowed entity.

There is the team, twelve players at home, or perhaps seventeen touring members away, coach Bob Simpson, media manager Ian McDonald and physiotherapist Errol Alcott. Wives and families, or girlfriends who become wives, are often relegated to backroom status – the occasional photograph or even article in a national women's magazine or newspaper, perhaps noting the birth of a new child. But the supportive, critical, rehabilitative role of any cricketer's wife should never be underestimated or downplayed.

So it is with Pip Boon.

David Boon has many fans around Australia and the world. Perhaps no other cricketer knows the intensity of being the *Test* player for Tasmania better than Boon, although in recent history both Roger Woolley and Greg Campbell have experienced the feeling.

Boon represents Tasmania in the Test arena to all of Australia and the rest of the world. Every Tasmanian seems to have an opinion about his last innings, his last series, the general state of his cricket – every aspect of his life, public or personal. The one person who bears the brunt of this, probably more than Boon himself, except when he is home in Launceston, is Pip and the members of David's immediate family.

Pip and David met when David was sixteen, attending Launceston Church Grammar School, and Pip was fifteen, going to Oakburn College (now a co-educational campus, Scotch Oakburn College), around the swimming pool at a friend's house. On Pip's twentieth birthday in 1982, they became engaged, having gone through two teenage 'break-ups' early in their relationship.

Pip jokes about David asking her father, Dr John Wright, for her hand in marriage. 'He didn't get an answer until about twelve months ago!' she said in 1992.

They were married at the Grammar School chapel and their honeymoon consisted of a holiday around Tasmania, touring the East Coast, down to the former convict prison at Port Arthur, Hobart and back to Launceston.

They were married in April. 'All cricketers get married in April,' David says. 'The Sheffield Shield and Australian seasons go from November to March and you're away from home. 'But it's far from normal. We've been married nine years and I've probably only spent four and a half years at home – it's almost a halfway house for me.'

Pip is one of five Wright women – her mother Patricia and sisters Alison, Rebecca, and Emma. Pip Boon is a strong, passionate person, who has never been afraid to speak her mind to or about David. She is generally wary of the media (as are most athletes and their partners) and in rare interviews, tends to make stock, non-committal comments. 'I'm a bit hesitant. I don't want to be seen to be whingeing or complaining,' Pip admits.

David's own stock comment about his wife is that while she understands and accepts the amount of time which a modern cricketer must spend away from home, she has never come to terms with it.

'No one can replace the company of your husband,' Pip states ' . . . You can try all you want to treat your friends or members of your family as a substitute, but it's not the same. Having said that, I would stress that I couldn't get by without my family or good friends. It's the loneliness, the constant loneliness. But then again, you can be your own worst enemy. You can't just sit at home and expect the world to come to you. It's up to you to keep busy.'

As David is Tasmania's sole Test cricketer, Pip has become her State's sole national cricketing wife. On the mainland, the network of Australian team and Sheffield Shield wives is entrenched in the system. Not so in Tasmania, where cricket exists in three regions – North, North-West and South – and, in 1991–92 at least, Boon was the only married player in the Shield team from Launceston, in Northern Tasmania.

'The girls in Western Australia have got a really good network,' Pip observes. 'On Sundays – those God-awful Sundays – they meet and go out to lunch or the cinema. It's a case of having and being with people in the same situation. At the very least, they have one other person to talk to. I've never had that – maybe that's why the phone bill is so enormous.'

With the Tasmanian public spotlight forever upon the Boon clan, Pip will admit that the anonymity of a Melbourne or Sydney would sometimes be preferable. When Australia plays Test cricket, much of the country monitors the national team's progress. In Tasmania in general, and Launceston specifically, the standard joke is that everything comes to a halt when Boon bats.

That pressure comes to rest squarely on Pip, because of Tasmania's size and lifestyle. People recognise and want, ninety-nine per cent for the best reasons, to pass on their opinions about David and wish him luck.

'Some people just can't help themselves, being honest,' Pip laughs. 'Most people are positive, but at times you can get quite defensive and be wounded by people's comments.'

The other side of the coin, being married to a 'famous' person, is that the partner's own personality and existence is reduced to that of a helpful appendage.

'Over the years I've tried my hardest just to be me,' Pip says. 'Many's the person I've bitten the head off because they've introduced me as David Boon's wife! I'm proud to be David's wife, but I want to be recognised as an individual too.'

David said that he has most noticed the strangeness of his existence in relation to their children – Georgina and Jack. 'I remember an occasion when Georgina was about twelve months old and I'd lift her out of the cot and she'd see me – this strange bloke – and start screaming hysterically. It was absolutely terrifying!'

David also noticed Georgina's early alienation on the Ashes tour of 1989 – he was separated from his family for 10 weeks before meeting up with them again at the Lord's Test. 'I put my arms out to take her and she grabbed hold of Pip,' Boon recalled. 'We took a walk, but it was only a very brief one. She wanted to go back to Pip. It hit hard to realise that your own daughter didn't really know you.'

Georgina has grown out of that stage, although she still dislikes his long absences. However, in recent seasons, her appreciation of cricket and his role has increased enormously. But Georgina can't understand one aspect of cricket. If Bruce Reid gets to bat, why doesn't her father get to bowl? 'For a period there, she thought I had my own plane,' David laughed.

'After kissing her goodnight, she'd ask me if I'd be home in the morning. Because quite often I come home for a night during the one-dayers. If I have to play a day-night match, I'll go on the early plane and when she wakes up I've gone.'

When he's on tour in Australia or overseas, Pip and David conduct their lives over the telephone. 'If we've both had a diabolical day, we'll explode on the phone,' Pip says. 'We're both stubborn and it's very hard to resolve anything on the phone in that frame of mind. But our whole marriage is conducted over the phone – decisions made, comparing and relating our experiences.'

But despite this downside, the fact that Pip has put her own career as a qualified nurse on hold and devoted herself to raising their family, largely unassisted because of David's schedule, she wouldn't change it.

'As gushy as it sounds, I'd prefer him to be away and happy than at home and miserable. I could never stand in the way of what he wants to do, just to have him at home. But there are times you think you'd swop it tomorrow.

'On the other hand, I have had the opportunity to travel to parts of the world that I might not have ever seen without cricket. I have made some very special friends because of cricket. There is never a dull or uninteresting moment in our lives!

'In analysing the constant separations, reunions and all the difficulties in between, I really believe that our relationship is stronger because of all that.'

One point of contention Pip has about cricket is that, in general, wives and families aren't welcome. There was minor controversy about the '89 tour of England, when wives were effectively banned until victory was achieved. David Boon spoke out against this measure in Australian team meetings during the tour lead-up, but when the final decision was made, he and Pip abided by the ruling.

'It's the nature of the game, a Test match,' David says. 'In five days, you are basically at the ground for ten, ten and a half hours a day. You become so single-minded, switched on to the day's play and what will happen tomorrow. People outside cricket speak to you and the brain doesn't recognise what's being said, because the brain is filled with what's important at the time.'

Boon admits that even in Australia, the cost of flying a cricketer's family to join him in Sydney or Melbourne is heavy. 'Having a family on tour is difficult,' Boon admits. 'But you have to put up with that if you want to see them. I don't see any problem with having "wives on tour". That's the environment from which you were originally selected for Australia. She's your wife – she's not going to cause a problem to your game.

'I do believe children on tour are more difficult. Young children's sleeping habits are different to an adult's, and they want to see their father at difficult times.'

Pip and Georgina went to England in 1989, but didn't stay at the Australian team's hotel – the 'no wives' rule banned that. David and Pip both believe that during longer tours – England is the longest – there should be period when the players travel alone. After that, wives and children should be welcome.

'The team could meet as the team half an hour each night before you go out to dinner,' Boon said. 'When you do out to dinner, whether in Australia or overseas, you rarely go out as a team. Three or four players might want to eat Chinese, three or four want to do this or do that – wives don't affect that, as long as your commitment is with the team and its goals. I believe that unnecessary separation creates unnecessary pressure.'

David and Pip know that his cricket career is the basis for future financial security for their family. But there is much more to their relationship. 'In a lot of instances in my career, I am positive that Pip has been the only person who could have got me through many of those tough periods,' David said. 'Geoff Marsh is the only other person who can pick me up when I'm really in a bad mood – Pip just does it immediately. She can get me out of it, because I'm not really a great communicator, particularly when things aren't going well.'

The other pressure for cricketers and their families is the spotlight that focuses on the players' lives on tour – whether it be in Australia or overseas. As a high-profile national entity, the Australian team, along with every other professional or semi-professional sporting team, is linked with rumours of wild lifestyle. One obvious example came after the 1991 Australian tour of West Indies, when the book *Calypso Cricket*, written by Sydney journalist Roland Fischman, was released.

Fischman's book, however it was viewed, contained two major allegations – that an Australian cricketer had slept with thirty different women and that another player had been 'entertaining' a woman in his room when his wife called. The Australian team closed ranks and refused to comment about the book.

Pip sees it from another viewpoint. 'Whether your husband is innocent or guilty, you're branded with the allegation,' Pip said. 'You've got to have trust. You'd go round the twist if you didn't have that trust. It does affect you because your husband's in that line of work – cricket and touring. But it happens in every line of work.'

One of the most difficult aspects of a cricketing family is the constant re-adjustment – Dad going off to play cricket, returning intermittently or not at all through the season, and then coming home for a lengthy stay in the off-season (if such a thing now exists on the Australian calendar).

'Many of the girls laugh about the fact that you have a pre-tour argument with your husband before he goes and a post-tour argument when he comes home,' Pip said. 'Then when he comes home, you've got this strange body in the house. You think, "This is my home, what are you doing here, disrupting my routine?"'

David contends that he is allowed seven days' settling-in. 'I come home and start throwing clothes everywhere,' David says. 'Pip lets me have a week before she says, "This is the cupboard, put your clothes in it. This is the dishwasher, put your dishes in it!"'

'But the children don't wait. You're used to looking after yourself in a hotel, doing things at your own pace. You can get up early and have a leisurely breakfast, or lie in bed late and rush to the ground. At home, things need to be done. Some things need to be done straight away and you've got to do them and think of something else and forget about the job at hand. But if the kids want you for something, they don't wait 15 minutes – they want you now!'

Pip just laughs. 'He sets his pace and that's the one that stays on the speedo,' Pip said. 'There can be a disaster in another room, but he'll just walk at the same pace to deal with it. This is the man with supposedly some of the quickest reflexes in cricket, who takes these unbelievably spectacular catches – but you look at him and he's so slow!'

'There's no point in rushing, really,' David says.

NEVILLE OLIVER ON BOON

Neville Oliver and David Boon are linked in life and cricket. Oliver, the ABC's federal head of Sport Radio, is a close friend of Boon's parents, Clarrie and Lesley, and watched young David grow up.

Oliver's first Test match as a cricket commentator coincided with Boon's first Test century – against India at the Adelaide Oval in 1985–86. Oliver was also sitting behind the microphone when Boon struck the winning runs on the glorious 4-0 Ashes tour of 1989. Oliver can recall a 19-year-old David Boon making his first Sheffield Shield century, and as a Tasmanian ABC Radio commentator, asking for an interview. The game was against Victoria at Hobart's TCA Ground in 1980–81.

'David honestly said, "I couldn't handle stuff like that,"' Oliver recalled. 'I told him that I thought he was going to be such a good player, he'd better used to it.'

Oliver is, for want of better terminology, a Boon Original. If most successful athletes or people have a hard-core of supporter-friends, Oliver is definitely in this category with Boon. His roots are with Boon's late father, Clarrie, and amateur football in Launceston.

'My relationship with his family is beyond Boon's memory,' Oliver said. 'I was close friends with Clarrie in the early 1960s when David was born. I watched David Boon at Charles St Primary School as a swimmer and an above average cricketer. And more so with Jack Simmons, whom I know extremely well, and who was the first to say that David had untold bags of ability. From Charles Street I saw him make a huge number of runs in the NTCA's Under-13 Week.'

Oliver is in many ways a larger-than-life character. When calling a Test match, one senses that Oliver has tremendous pride in his country's players. His detractors nearly always say he is too close to his subject. But the general listener appreciates Oliver's insight and rapport with the Australian players.

It was once stated to Boon that Oliver simply carries on too much about the conversations that he had with this Greg Chappell or that Ian Chappell. Boon smiled and replied that Oliver at least did all the things he talked about – he spoke the truth.

Above all, Oliver is passionate about sport – all sorts – and his friends. Tasmanian legend says that a detractor once entered an ABC broadcast box for a bit of one-on-one criticism. Oliver unceremoniously deposited the man outside.

Oliver is in a special position with Boon – both friend and sometime critic – one which he honestly treasures. 'To see a young child grow up to become a Test player is quite amazing,' Oliver said. 'Australia has a population of 17 million, but only eleven Test players at one time. The chances of being able to see a Test player from a very early age are therefore exceptionally limited. And not many would have been sports commentators, calling his progress.

'I have watched Boon grow up, score his first Test century against India and develop into a great Test player. It is a very rare relationship.'

Oliver also sat behind the microphone for one of Boon's biggest disappointments – his innings of 94 against England in the third Test at Lord's in 1989. Boon has never made a secret of the fact that a century in England, particularly at Lord's, would be one of his career highlights.

'So there we were at Lord's, me calling the game, and of all players, David was in his 90s,' Oliver said. 'Then he played the worst shot he has played for several years! I can fully understand how he must have felt, because I'll bet my own feelings weren't dissimilar. To come so close at Lord's must have been almost soul-destroying.'

Oliver said that because of the enormity of that near-miss, he knew Boon well enough to steer clear of him for any extended conversation.

However, Oliver believes that Boon has certainly come to terms with the vagaries of success and failure in Test cricket. 'In his early days, when David scored noughts and 49s, he tended to wear the disappointment on his sleeve. Now, as he has become more of a fixture in Australian cricket, he is less inclined to show his emotions, because he knows that a cricketer is judged across the whole array of his career – first-class, one-day and Test matches.'

Oliver watched from the ABC commentary box the Australian season of 1986–87, when Boon struggled against England – despite a century in Adelaide – and was dropped from the Test team. 'There were probably doubts about his ability in '86–87 when he forgot where his off-stump was and gave various slips cordons catching practice, and finally lost his place,' Oliver said.

'But there is still a smattering of the cricket legend, "Thou shalt never be judged on what you are doing now, but thou shalt be judged by what you were doing when you were young". Boon's Test average is now between 40 and 50 and the best judges that I speak to, the Tony Coziers, the Christopher Martin-Jenkins and the Jonathon Agnews, regard him as one of the best around.'

Oliver noted that with Boon's tally of Test centuries standing at

14 after the 1992–93 Australian season and New Zealand tour, his final position in world cricket is yet to be realised. 'He has an extraordinarily healthy record. Thirteen Test hundreds stand up against anyone except those who have been knighted,' Oliver said. 'He has already gone past some massively good, international cricketers. But Boon has the potential to play another three years at international level. A David Boon with 20 Test hundreds would be remembered as one of the game's greats.'

Oliver has also witnessed the extraordinary pressure – particularly in Tasmania – under which Boon has played. Boon has been feted in his home town of Launceston since he started making centuries as a 12-year-old, but the attention definitely increased when as a 16-year-old he was selected for the Australia Under-19 tour of England in 1977.

'Boon didn't play Test cricket until 1984,' Oliver said. 'And playing for Tasmania, as a terrific player in an ordinary side, he got a lot more press than a mediocre player in a good side.

'But he had to prove himself to be a little bit special to be a Test player. It was a double-edged sword. It was hard to make it initially, but he made it because he got a lot of press. Boon got rave reviews for a 50 for Tasmania, when a New South Wales player in the same situation might not have.

'The biggest favour ever done to him was that he was 24 years old when he made the Test team. Look at all the players who were raced into Test cricket, failed, and were never heard from again. When Boon made the Test team, he was ready to take the next step.'

Oliver said that Boon has adapted to and handled extremely well the pressure and adulation that goes with being an Australian cricketer. 'For a bloke who has achieved what he has in sport, he has changed very, very little. If anything now, he is a bit more open and confident of his place in life.

'I find through my own sporting life as a commentator, interviewing and talking to some extremely famous sporting people, that the greatest retain that touch of humility. They are very well-adjusted people. Generally speaking, the insufferable bores of this world are the ones who have huge ideas about their abilities and have never actually achieved what their egos tell them they should have.'

Oliver said that he has observed an interesting phenomenon in recent Australian domestic seasons – the adoption/acceptance of Boon by the vast majority of fans around the country. 'He's become to Australian fans what he always meant to Tasmania. When Boon has walked out the gate for Tasmania, the fans' hopes have been on his shoulders and obviously more times than not he has delivered, just by looking at his Shield average. He has demonstrated that he has been Australia's best player in the past two or three years – and now when he walks out onto the MCG, SCG and the WACA Ground, there is a special magic that exists between the crowd and Boon.

'He has transcended State boundaries, like an Allan Border – he is an *Australian* cricketer, rather than the boy from Tassie. It's very special to hear a capacity crowd at the SCG give him a rally which they normally reserve for their own.'

Oliver said that Boon was one of the wits of the Australian team, a man renowned for his dry sense of humour. However, Oliver says that he still loses his temper when people describe Boon as arrogant. 'If you want to get me angry, just tell me he's arrogant – he's just not,' Oliver said. 'David Boon is a shy person. But people will swear to me, people who have never met him or even been in the same town as him, that he's arrogant. He certainly has the walk of a small man, the swagger, but that's just his roly-poly walk, because of his roly-poly build.

'Boon can get a laugh out of most blokes and he can laugh at himself, even when he's down. Boon is one cricketer who stared the bloke who was a failure in the face and came back.'

It is Boon's characteristic swagger and status on the subcontinent, particularly India, that allows Oliver to tell a typically, irreverent story about his friend.

'He thought he was adored in India. Whenever he came out to bat, the crowd would chant 'Boon, Boon, Boon' and he would swagger just that little bit more,' Oliver said. 'But in Punjabi, Boon, or a word very close, means 'arsehole'. So the crowd could have been chanting something with completely different connotations.

'I told Boon that and I don't think he was even vaguely amused!'

MIKE GATTING ON BOON

What a difference a year makes. That's what was going through my mind after David had just saved Australia from possible defeat in the Bicentennial Test match in Sydney in 1988. He has since gone from strength to strength.

In the Bicentennial Test, he scored a magnificent 184 and batted through the five sessions left – one day and two hours. He did have a bit of assistance, the weather and bad light in Sydney. The question was asked, I might add in a light-hearted way, 'Why can't we have the floodlights on?'

Nevertheless, 'Boon the Brave' was in stark contrast to 'Give Boon the Boot' in 1986–87. The 1986–87 series was a sad one for David, though he might actually use different words. He scored 144 runs in a total of eight innings with 103 at Adelaide contributing the bulk of the runs.

I spoke with David occasionally, and we seemed to get on quite well, although people used to say that it was because of our similar girths. He was very down at the end of the fourth Test, but I always sensed that determination in him to succeed. His fears that he would be dropped for the fifth Test were confirmed.

Then the great Taylor debate began – was it Peter or Mark? To this day, I can't believe that Australia would go into a Test match without two recognised openers – that's of course meant to be no disrespect to Greg Ritchie.

David's worries were numerous, as they are when you're not playing well, when, in fact, one or two little things put right might cure all – well, almost all. David got a very good delivery from Neil Foster during the first innings of the Bicentennial Test and with our boys bowling well we managed to make Australia follow-on. It was then that we saw the emergence of the new David Boon, which many sides were to witness in the years that followed: a solid, broad, moustached, confident opener.

It was a great temptation this year, 1992, to take up the offer to play for Tasmania along with David. Not only for the cricket, but to play that long-awaited game of snooker and round of golf, not to mention the beer David's been promising me for ages.

SIR RICHARD HADLEE ON BOON

My first encounter with David Boon was in 1979, when I first played for Tasmania as an overseas professional. He was only 16 or 17 at the time and many people felt that he would play for Tasmania that year because of his exciting potential and proven performances in under-age cricket.

I recall bowling to him in the indoor nets of the NTCA Ground, under the watchful eye of many, including his father, Clarrie. I guess I was expected to bowl 'Daniel' out and test him to see what he was really made of – maybe that practice session was his first trial to see whether he was good enough to play for Tassie.

David certainly coped with the situation very well. He looked to be a very well-organised batsman, particularly at his age, bearing in mind his lack of experience. He was picked for Tasmania that year and, under the circumstances, played well, as the team didn't have a great season.

'Daniel' used to score a lot of 20s and 30s and there were doubts as to whether he could turn those types of scores into big ones and eventually play for Australia. I certainly felt he was good enough and thought it would be an interesting twist of fate if we were to battle against each other in the Test arena.

He used to go for his shots and play aggressively, as most youngsters like to do. If one is prepared to play that way, there is an element of risk and mistakes can be made by being over-confident. I feel David was a little like that, but that is all part of a cricketer's early development and experience. However, if a player is to achieve the ultimate, he has to eliminate these mistakes and learn to play within his limitations. The true test was to follow.

The 1985–86 Test series in Australia was New Zealand's ultimate performance. We had never beaten Australia in Australia and probably didn't expect to either – nothing had really changed within our team structure except that we had Glenn Turner as our cricket manager-coach. Turner's influence should never be underestimated because his vast knowledge was invaluable.

New Zealand were prepared better than ever before, both physically and mentally – we were ready to do battle at the 'Gabba. Glenn had spent some time with me in the nets, trying to get me to bowl closer to the stumps, so that when I delivered I was bowling stump to stump, causing the batsmen more problems – they had to play the balls more frequently. If the ball moved away, there was a chance of a nick to the slips; if the ball seamed back, there was the chance of a leg before wicket or bowled dismissal. Obviously, I would give myself more options of dismissing any batsman.

As it turned out, Australia went into bat in ideal bowling conditions, and was dismissed for 172. I had career-best figures of 9–52. There was a possibility of capturing all 10 wickets, but I mucked that up by catching Geoff Lawson off Vaughan Brown – his first Test wicket!

I always felt that if I could get the ball to move in the air and off the seam, the Aussie batsmen would struggle. Generally, Australian players like to play off the back foot and from the crease – if the ball moved there was a greater margin for error and for the batsman to be caught out of position.

My total of 33 wickets in the series certainly gave me a psychological advantage and an ascendancy over the Australians.

In the first innings of the first Test, I had David Boon caught at slip by Jeremy Coney. 'Daniel' pushed at a ball outside off-stump – he often fended or sparred at deliveries in that area. David tended to square up on the crease, so I had various options available.

My simple theory to bowling was consistency – line and length on or about off-stump, committing the batsmen to play. I would 'interrogate' the batsmen by probing away relentlessly, asking him: 'Can you play this delivery? Can you play that delivery?' Wherever I pitched the ball affected an outcome – maiden delivery, runs scored or wicket taken. I always wanted to try and dominate the batsman, but I'm realistic enough to know that a batsman on his day would dominate me in return.

New Zealand won that first Test by an innings – a remarkable performance. Martin Crowe and John Reid scored centuries for New Zealand and six more wickets for me in the second innings caused the victory.

However, it was a different situation in the second Test at the Sydney Cricket Ground – Australia wanted to square the series with one more to play in Perth. I had David lbw for a duck in Sydney and he was under pressure to score runs in the second innings, otherwise his Test career may well have ended for a period of time. A fighting 81 saved his spot, but also provided a morale-boosting victory for Australia.

The third Test allowed me to dismiss David twice more – caught by John Bracewell in slip for 12 and bowled for 50. New Zealand won the Test match to clinch the series 2–1, our first-ever series victory against Australia in Australia.

David and I were having some good battles – I had won the first confrontation because I worked out a strategy. In 1987, the return to the 'Gabba gave New Zealand great confidence to repeat history. One man changed that – David Boon. His 143, run out, was a magnificent performance, one of many to follow in his career. David had worked out a way of playing me that reduced my effectiveness. His plan was quite simple – play at the balls that he had to and let the rest go. By his concentrating harder, the bowler is worn down, becomes frustrated and bowls a bit straighter. Whenever I bowled straighter, 'Daniel' was able to dispatch me through mid-wicket and mid-on for many runs. My figures of 3–95 were vastly different from 9–52.

Another thing which frustrated me a little was David and Geoff 'Swampy' Marsh's understanding when running between wickets – they kept taking cheeky singles, which not only kept the scoreboard ticking over, but the strike was changed and the bowler's plan and rhythm upset.

In the second Test in Adelaide, I had to change my plan again because of David's marvellous success. He was probably overjoyed, feeling he had squared our private battle. I opted to alternate my delivery pattern. Instead of bowling close to the wicket as my stock delivery, I felt I had to bowl wide of the crease so that I was angling it more at off-stump. Therefore it would be difficult for David to let the ball go outside off-stump if I was fractionally wide. I didn't want to bowl too straight at middle stump because David would have again been severe in his toll through mid-on and mid-wicket. I had success – David played one on for six. In the third Test in Melbourne, I trapped him lbw for 10, so perhaps the battle was even again.

There was never any 'aggro', ill-feeling or verbal confrontation. There was just a nod, a wink, a glare or perhaps a smile as we both got on with the business at hand. I dismissed him eight times in my Test career – he scored his share of runs.

I think there was a lot of respect between us and our friendship will always continue.

JACK SIMMONS ON BOON

The first time I ever set eyes on David Boon was as a coach for one of many schools allocated to me under a scheme for under-13 players I had organised for the Northern Tasmanian Cricket

Association. There was one youngster who stood head and shoulders above the rest – David Boon. And it wasn't just that year in Northern Tasmania, where I coached at 36 schools, but David was the best 10-year-old I had seen in Tasmania, England or my previous contracted coaching in South Africa.

David's natural ability was evident, but what was a breath of fresh air was his will to want to be in the game. Although he was still so very young, I told David that he had talent and I would like to help him bring it to fruition. David's immediate reply was that he played and enjoyed other sports – Australian Rules and swimming specifically. David was like every other youngster at that age, keen to take part in everything.

My next cricket program for the NTCA involved the best under-13s, for more advanced coaching. It called for the boys to be available on Fridays, Saturdays, even Sundays – they knew their enthusiasm and ability were appreciated. I wanted David to be a part of this and approached his parents, Clarrie and Lesley, to make sure he would participate. I think I convinced them of the natural ability that David possessed. His parents were obviously keen to see David develop and I knew that whenever or wherever I wanted him to attend, they would get him there.

Even in a program which selected the best pupils of all the Northern Tasmanian schools, David still surpassed others his age.

I initiated an Under-13 Cricket Week, so that schools played games on the NTCA Ground and the NTCA No. 2 Ground. David scored a century on the NTCA Ground when he was 12, competing against 13-year-olds. His innings illustrated the determination, dedication and concentration that he possessed.

David Boon progressed from his primary school, Launceston's Charles St, to Launceston Church Grammar School on a scholarship. We became friends, not just in a teacher–pupil relationship, but because of mutual respect and admiration for one another; as far I was concerned, he was like a son to me. At that time, I had no children at all, and even now I regard him in a very special way.

David was again head and shoulders above his age group at Grammar, even in its privileged set-up. I had progressed to coaching at the private schools – Grammar, Scotch College (now Scotch Oakburn College) and St Patrick's College – but continued to oversee David's direction.

David joined the Launceston Cricket Club and stayed with the Lions through all the different age groups – under-13, 14, 15 and 16. His cricket progressed in leaps and bounds, and at 16 he was a member of the Tasmanian Under-18 team.

The following year, he was captain, leading the team to the national carnival. I was a little disappointed because David suffered a couple of rough decisions and unlucky dismissals during the games. But he won selection in a trial game for the first Australian Under-19 schoolboy tour of England.

David, because of his scores, couldn't be guaranteed a place in the first XI, but he made it into the second XI. He was looked upon as a reserve, and didn't go in to bat until number 12 – they were batting to 12 – and by that time his side wasn't in a good position. David walked out onto the Melbourne Cricket Ground and scored a century! It was definitely the right away to impress the right people at the right time. David was selected for the prestigious tour.

As I was still playing for Lancashire, I very much wanted to see him play. But I was, however, prevented by the fixtures, with most games played south of Birmingham and not at Lancashire, Nottinghamshire, Leicestershire or Darbyshire. However, Colin Cowdrey later told me that the tour was arranged at considerable speed and that the main sponsors were based there.

David had a good if not outstanding tour, but his dedication, will to learn and desire to make cricket his career were impressive.

When David returned home, he won his Tasmanian cap at the age of 17. I don't think there was a prouder man than myself – I was then Tasmanian captain. He made his debut in a one-day game, the semi-final of the Gillette Cup (now the FAI Cup) against

Queensland in Brisbane. And he won the game for Tasmania!

Batting with a number 11, a lad called Gary Whitney, David was still out there when Tasmania needed about 10 runs to win. Phil Carlson had the last over of the semi-final and he bowled David a bouncer. He hit it in front of square on the deck and the resulting boundary gave us victory. Tasmania went on to beat Western Australia in the 1978–79 Gillette Cup final.

Throughout one's cricket career, people often ask about your best innings, best bowling performance, best catches, best victory. Naturally, you have great memories and satisfaction from years of professional cricket. As a coach, you receive similar – often greater – satisfaction from watching a youngster, whom you have helped, progress and succeed. Watching David Boon in his first game for Tasmania was one of my greatest highlights. It was the manner in which he took on the responsibility to win the match – a task which should have gone to a player of more experience and maturity. From that day on, I knew David was destined not just to be a top-class player for Tasmania, but also for Australia.

In his early days, I know that I went out on a limb and said to various people that if David continued to progress at the same rate he would represent his country. But I just felt that this lad would do it. I am pleased to say that David has surpassed all my expectations and that he has never disappointed me, in any way, on or off the field. His feats for Tasmania and Australia have since been well-documented. However, it was in the Australian summer of 1991–92 that I felt he began to receive the acclaim from the media that should have been his long before.

David Boon is now regarded as not only one of the best batsmen in Australia, but also the world. And having spoken to David's best mate, Geoff Marsh, I know that he has remained a great team man. My philosophy has always been that team spirit – whether playing for Tasmania or a County or League side in the United Kingdom – is first and foremost.

In the super league of international Test cricket, receiving the superstardom which goes with being in the elite can make being a team man difficult. Because of the money and the publicity spotlight, team-work and spirit can be forgotten and replaced by the promotion of individuals. However, one reason I am proud of David, his achievements and the heights he has reached, is that he still believes in the team principles. Whether in Tasmania or the rest of Australia, David still finds time to have an ale and a chat with the mates who were his mates at school, his club team-mates and opponents and State players.

David has never forgotten his background or the people who helped him when he was on the way up. When I left Tasmania in 1983, knowing that I would not return as coach or as a player, David told me that if he had a son, he would name him after me. It was very generous of him to make such a remark, but I didn't think anything would come of it. But when Pip gave birth to their second child and it was a boy, David telephoned and said, 'I would like to call him Jack, would you mind?' as well as asking me to be his son's godfather.

As a player I have enjoyed many great thrills in my lifetime – Tasmania's Gillette Cup victory, even being awarded an MBE by the Queen. But to have a baby named after you, by someone whom you regard as a son, is truly amazing. I felt that everything I had tried to instill in David, as a promising cricketer and man, had been appreciated.

When I put the phone down after David's call, I was overcome with emotion – the same feeling that occurred when David's father, Clarrie, rang and told me he had been selected for Australia in his first Test match against the West Indies in Brisbane in 1984–85. Tears welled in my eyes on both occasions as I turned to tell my wife Jacqueline what had happened. I had always promised myself that if David was selected for Australia, I would watch his debut. Unfortunately, if I had honoured that personal pledge, I would have let down two leagues to which I had promised to present trophies and other cricketing engagements on the Thursday and Friday nights of that Test match.

I did contemplate leaving England on Saturday and arriving in Australia on the Monday. But I also faced not seeing any play because of the dominance of the West Indian combination. As it turned out, the game finished in four days. But I was highly delighted that David scored a half-century in his second innings.

In the next couple of years, people throughout Australia began to realise David's talent and offers were made by other states to him to move, as many players have done in the past – Sir Donald Bradman, Allan Border, Jeff Thomson among them. The temptation was the opportunity for greater remuneration and recognition playing for the bigger states. Fortunately, because of the motivation and intelligence of certain people in cricket and business circles in Northern Tasmanian, David was persuaded not to leave.

The rest is history – the depth of feeling in which David is regarded by the Tasmanian people was part-way explained when the main grandstand at the NTCA Ground was named after him in 1991–92.

Long may he continue to grace grounds, not just in Tasmania, but in Australia and the rest of the world for many years to come.

POSTSCRIPT

*O*n Friday 12 February 1993, one of David Boon's greatest-
ever fans – his father Clarrie – died. Mr Boon had fought a
battle for several years with lung cancer, his spirits continually
buoyed by his family, his wife Lesley, children David and Vanessa
and grandchildren Georgina and Jack.

On Tuesday 16 February, the day after Mr Boon's funeral in
Launceston, this article appeared in the Examiner, written by the
author.

OBITUARY   The *Examiner*'s sports news editor Mark Thomas salutes
the passing of Mr Clarrie Boon, whose funeral was held in Launceston
yesterday.

When Sheffield Shield Cricket was played at the NTCA Ground,
I would meet him under the shady trees of the eastern flank of
the oval. From there, where you can seemingly reach out and touch

the players in the middle, we would talk: cricket was understandably in season, but football was never far away.

Often we would talk about his son, David Boon, who was either on-field or elsewhere around Australia wielding the willow. There was always understandable pride in Mr Clarrie Boon's voice when the subject of David was raised, but also a serious modesty, a straightforwardness in discussing performance and form.

I recall standing in a luncheon tent packed with cricket fans, during a Shield match, men in white in the middle and the Australian team in action on the television screen. David was given out leg before wicket and someone called out, 'What about that one, Clarrie?' He simply replied, 'It's in the scorebook, isn't it?' – a rhetorical statement that complaint was useless.

From a distance, whether at the cricket in Launceston, Hobart, Melbourne or Sydney, Clarrie was unmistakable, his build and gait the more mature version of his son's signature stroll to the wicket.

Clarrie and Lesley were at Lord's when David made 94 in the first innings, but they rate his 58 not out in the second, steering Australia to victory as one of his finest hands. The team always comes first for a Boon.

The first time I recall meeting Clarrie I tried to call him 'Mr Boon'. 'Call me Clarrie', however, was his constant rejoinder.

As a first- or second-year reporter in the mid eighties, I was dispatched by my editor to discuss amateur football in Launceston, where players were 'allegedly' paid vast sums of money. Shock! Horror! thought I, having pulled on the Lilywhite boot in Melbourne. I think I held the high moral ground, but I never had a chance. 'I always checked my boot after a good game, just in case,' he said with a wry grin.

He abhorred football violence, not blokes banging heads, necessarily, but bullies picking on weaker players.

In recent years, we spoke often of recording David Boon's cricket career. Clarrie had done the groundwork, collecting seemingly every piece of information about his famed son – centuries, ducks, the lot – from newspapers, magazines, photographs and video-tapes. There were 27 scrapbooks of priceless material and in his last weeks, he requested the final volume be returned so that he could continue his work.

I would publicly state that without Clarrie Boon, there would be no book in its current format, because of his diligence and love for his son.

But in talking to Clarrie for the proposed work, his own influence on the younger Boon was continually understated, stressing the importance of David's mother, Lesley Boon, the former Australian hockey vice-captain, upon David's development.

Mrs Boon was the first to point out that Clarrie was the one to drive David to training – every morning swimming as a young boy with the South Esk club and to every practice session with Jack Simmons – as he did with his daughter Vanessa for horse riding and hockey.

Clarrie Boon was a formidable sports administrator, but, first and always, he was husband, father and grandfather to his family.

Vale, Clarrie. I shall miss talking to you at the cricket.

DC BOON
STATISTICAL PROFILE
(to 1 May 1993)

REPRESENTATIVE CRICKET

	M	Inns	NO	HS	Runs	Aver.	100	50	Ca
First-Class	206	349	32	227	14503	45.75	42	67	176
Sheff.Shield	78	137	4	227	5588	42.02	15	27	65
Test	74	135	14	200	5314	43.92	14	24	73
Tas. 1-Day	40	38	1	94	1274	34.43	0	11	11
L.O. Int	139	135	10	122	4428	35.42	5	25	35

ALL FIRST-CLASS CRICKET

	M	Inns	NO	HS	Runs	Aver.	100	50	Ca
1978–79	2	3	0	22	34	11.33	0	0	2
1979–80	7	13	1	90	404	33.66	0	3	3
1980–81	7	13	0	114	518	39.84	1	3	6
1981–82	7	13	2	88	473	43.00	0	3	4
1982–83	12	18	1	115	682	40.11	2	3	8
1982–83 (Zim)	2	3	0	148	274	91.33	2	0	3
1983–84	11	19	0	227	667	35.10	1	4	8
1984–85	10	18	2	147	664	41.50	3	2	8
1985 (Eng)	15	20	5	206*	832	55.46	3	3	13
1985–86	9	17	1	196	818	51.12	3	3	3
1985–86 (NZ)	4	7	1	109	302	50.33	1	2	2
1986–87 (Ind)	6	8	1	122	476	68.00	1	3	4
1986–87	13	26	0	172	821	31.57	3	1	8
1987–88	12	21	2	184*	1287	67.73	5	6	13
1988–89 (Pak)	5	8	0	76	258	32.25	0	2	11
1988–89	13	23	2	149	939	44.71	2	6	13
1989 (Eng)	17	28	5	151	1306	56.78	3	8	21
1989–90	8	14	2	200	657	54.75	3	1	6
1989–90 (NZ)	1	2	0	12	12	6.00	0	0	0
1990–91	9	17	2	121	809	53.93	2	4	10
1990–91 (WI)	10	14	1	109*	456	35.07	2	2	6
1991–92	10	16	2	135	819	58.50	4	1	11
1992–93 (SL)	5	9	0	68	235	26.11	0	2	3
1992–93	8	15	2	111	635	48.84	1	4	7
1992–93 (NZ)	3	4	0	53	125	31.25	0	1	3
	206	349	32	227	14503	45.75	42	67	176

First-Class Record By Opponents

	M	Inns	NO	HS	Runs	Aver.	100	50	Ca
Aus states	78	137	4	227	5588	42.02	15	27	65
Eng teams	46	75	14	206*	3317	54.37	10	15	39
WI teams	29	49	6	149	1725	40.11	4	9	25
Ind teams	15	24	4	135	1418	70.90	6	5	13
NZ teams	17	29	2	200	1223	45.30	4	6	15
Pak teams	9	15	0	76	403	26.86	0	2	12
SL teams	10	17	2	133*	555	37.00	1	4	4
Zim teams	2	3	0	148	274	91.33	2	0	3
	206	349	32	227	14503	45.75	42	68	176

First-Class Record By Country

	M	Inns	NO	HS	Runs	Aver.	100	50	Ca
In Aus	138	246	19	227	10227	45.05	30	44	110
In Eng	32	48	10	206*	2138	56.26	6	11	34
In NZ	8	13	1	109	439	36.58	1	3	5
In Ind	6	8	1	122	476	68.00	1	3	4
In Pak	5	8	0	76	258	32.25	0	2	11
In WI	10	14	1	109*	456	35.07	2	2	6
In Zim	2	3	0	148	274	91.33	2	0	3
In SL	5	9	0	68	235	26.11	0	2	3
	206	349	32	227	14503	45.75	42	67	176

FIRST-CLASS RECORD BY GROUND

	M	Inns	NO	HS	Runs	Aver.	100	50	Ca
Brisbane	16	28	1	143	1055	39.07	4	4	15
Sydney	15	29	3	184*	1405	54.03	5	5	13
Melbourne	15	28	2	227	1057	40.65	2	4	4
Launceston	14	26	1	172	1172	46.88	4	4	11
TCA	15	24	3	196	978	46.57	3	3	6
Bellerive	10	18	1	108	692	40.70	2	4	7
Devonport	16	27	4	133*	1093	47.52	2	5	14
Adelaide	17	31	3	135	1420	50.71	6	5	14
Perth	19	34	1	200	1326	40.18	2	10	16
St Kilda	1	1	0	29	29	29.00	0	0˙	0
Totals:	138	246	19	227	10227	45.05	30	44	110

FIRST-CLASS RECORD, HOME VS AWAY (1)

	M	Inns	NO	HS	Runs	Aver.	100	50	Ca
Tas.	39	68	5	196	2842	45.11	9	11	24
Mainland	99	178	14	227	7385	45.03	21	33	86
Overseas	68	103	13	206*	4276	47.51	12	23	66
	206	349	32	227	14503	45.75	42	67	176

First-Class Record, Home vs Away (2)

	M	Inns	NO	HS	Runs	Aver.	100	50	Ca
In Aus	138	246	19	227	10227	45.05	30	44	110
Overseas	68	103	13	206*	4276	47.51	12	23	66
	206	349	32	227	14503	45.75	42	67	176

Tasmanian First-Class Record

	M	Inns	NO	HS	Runs	Aver.	100	50	Ca
1978–79	2	3	0	22	34	11.33	0	0	2
1978–79	2	3	0	22	34	11.33	0	0	2
1979–80	7	13	1	90	404	33.66	0	3	3
1980–81	7	13	0	114	518	39.84	1	3	6
1981–82	7	13	2	88	473	43.00	0	3	4
1982–83	12	18	1	115	682	40.11	2	3	8
1983–84	11	19	0	227	667	35.10	1	4	8
1984–85	7	13	2	147	532	48.36	3	1	6
1985–86	3	5	0	196	320	64.00	1	1	1
1986–87	9	18	0	172	677	37.61	2	1	7
1987–88	7	13	1	143	790	65.83	3	4	7
1988–89	8	13	1	132	542	45.16	1	4	4
1989–90	3	5	2	133*	335	111.66	2	1	3
1990–91	3	6	0	33	104	17.33	0	0	6
1991–92	4	6	0	130	253	42.16	1	0	3
1992–93	2	3	0	60	106	35.33	0	1	1
	92	161	10	227	6437	42.62	17	29	69

SHEFFIELD SHIELD RECORD

	M	Inns	NO	HS	Runs	Aver.	100	50	Ca
1978–79	2	3	0	22	34	11.33	0	0	2
1979–80	5	9	0	90	257	28.55	0	2	2
1980–81	5	10	0	114	428	42.80	1	2	5
1981–82	5	9	1	88	329	41.12	0	3	4
1982–83	10	15	1	115	589	42.06	2	3	8
1983–84	10	18	0	227	660	36.66	1	4	8
1984–85	6	11	1	147	499	49.90	3	1	5
1985–86	3	5	0	196	320	64.00	1	1	1
1986–87	8	16	0	172	646	40.37	2	1	7
1987–88	6	11	0	143	645	58.63	2	4	6
1988–89	7	12	1	132	541	49.18	1	4	4
1989–90	2	3	0	100	177	59.00	1	1	3
1990–91	3	6	0	33	104	17.33	0	0	6
1991–92	4	6	0	130	253	42.16	1	0	3
1992–93	2	3	0	60	106	35.33	0	1	1
	78	137	4	227	5588	42.02	5	27	65

First-Class Record By State Opponent

	M	Inns	NO	HS	Runs	Aver.	100	50	Ca
NSW	15	26	2	196	1052	43.83	3	4	13
Qld	17	29	1	172	1251	44.67	6	3	17
SA	14	25	0	130	973	38.92	2	5	10
Vic.	14	23	0	227	1109	48.22	3	5	10
WA	18	34	1	147	1203	36.45	1	10	15
	78	137	4	227	5588	42.02	15	27	65

Centuries In First-Class Cricket
(*capitals refer to Test match scores)

Score	For	Versus*	Venue	Season
114	Tas	Vic.	TCA	1980–81
115	Tas	Qld	Brisbane	1982–83
109	Tas	SA	Adelaide	1982–83
148	YAus	Zim	Harare	1982–83
108	YAus	Zim	Harare	1982–83
227	Tas	Vic	MCG	1983–84
138	Tas	NSW	L'ton	1984–85
104	Tas	Vic.	MCG	1984–85
147	Tas	WA	TCA	1984–85
119	Aus	Suss	Hove	1985
138	Aus	Ess	Chelmsford	1985
206*	Aus	Northants	Northampton	1985
196	Tas	NSW	TCA	1985–86
123	AUS	IND	ADELAIDE	1985–86
131	AUS	IND	SYDNEY	1985–86

continues next page

CENTURIES IN FIRST-CLASS CRICKET continued

Score	For	Versus*	Venue	Season
109	Aus	CenDis	New Plymouth	1985-86
122	AUS	IND	MADRAS	1986-87
117	Tas	Qld	Brisbane	1986-87
103	AUS	ENG	ADELAIDE	1986-87
172	Tas	Qld	L'ton	1986-87
143	AUS	NZ	BRISBANE	1987-88
101*	Tas	NZ	D'port	1987-88
184*	AUS	ENG	SYDNEY	1987-88
108	Tas	Qld	L'ton	1987-88
143	Tas	Qld	L'ton	1987-88
149	AUS	WI	SYDNEY	1988-89
132	Tas	NSW	Sydney	1988-89
103	Aus	Hants	Southampton	1989
102*	Aus	Northants	Northampton	1989
151	Aus	Ess.	Chelmsford	1989
100	Tas	Qld	Bellerive	1989-90
200	AUS	NZ	PERTH	1989-90
133*	Tas	SL	D'port	1989-90
108	Aus	Eng	Bellerive	1990-91
121	AUS	ENG	ADELAIDE	1990-91
105	Aus	Jam	Kingston	1990-91
109*	AUS	WI	KINGSTON	1990-91
130	Tas	SA	Adelaide	1991-92
129*	AUS	IND	SYDNEY	1991-92
135	AUS	IND	ADELAIDE	1991-92
107	AUS	IND	PERTH	1991-92
111	AUS	WI	BRISBANE	1992-93

CENTURY PARTNERSHIPS IN FIRST-CLASS CRICKET
(*capitals refer to Test match scores)

Wkt	P'ship	For	Partner	Versus*	Venue	Season
1	217	AUS	GR MARSH	IND	SYDNEY	1985–86
1	195	Tas	EJ Harris	Qld	Brisbane	1986–87
1	162	AUS	GR MARSH	ENG	SYDNEY	1987–88
1	145	Tas	N Jelich	Qld	L'ton	1986–87
1	138	Aus	GR Marsh	Patron XI	Lahore	1988–89
1	129	Aus	GR Marsh	NWFP XI	Peshawar	1988–89
1	126	Tas	GA Hughes	Qld	L'ton	1987–88
1	124	Tas	GA Hughes	Qld	L'ton	1987–88
1	121	Tas	GA Hughes	Vic	L'ton	1988–89
1	120	AUS	GR MARSH	SL	PERTH	1987–88
1	117*	AUS	MA TAYLOR	WI	SYDNEY	1992–93
1	116	Aus	GR Marsh	Pres XI	Bangalore	1986–87
1	113	AUS	GR MARSH	ENG	ADELAIDE	1986–87
1	108	Tas	GA Hughes	WA	Bellerive	1988–89
1	104	AUS	GR MARSH	NZ	WELLINGTON	1985–86
2	221	AUS	MA TAYLOR	IND	ADELAIDE	1991–92
2	192*	Tas	G Shipperd	SL	D'port	1989–90
2	167	Aus	TM Moody	Ess	Chelmsford	1989
2	166	Tas	G Shipperd	Qld	Bellerive	1989–90
2	158	AUS	DM JONES	IND	MADRAS	1986–87
2	156	Tas	BA Cruse	SA	Adelaide	1991–92
2	149	AUS	TM MOODY	NZ	PERTH	1989–90
2	146	Aus	AR Border	Midd	Lord's	1989
2	145	AUS	MA TAYLOR	ENG	LORD'S	1989
2	142	Tas	M Ray	WA	L'ton	1983–84
2	121	Tas	M Ray	Vic	MCG	1984–85
2	118	AUS	SR WAUGH	WI	SYDNEY	1992–93
2	111	AUS	MA TAYLOR	WI	BRIDGETOWN	1990–91

continues next page

CENTURY PARTNERSHIPS IN FIRST-CLASS CRICKET continued

Wkt	P'ship	For	Partner	Versus*	Venue	Season
2	110	Aus	MA Taylor	Som	Taunton	1989
2	106	AUS	MA TAYLOR	IND	MCG	1991-92
2	105	AUS	WB PHILLIPS	NZ	SYDNEY	1985-86
2	105	Tas	J Cox	NSW	Sydney	1988-89
2	105	Tas	RF Jeffery	Pak	L'ton	1981-82
2	102	Aus	MA Taylor	Hamp	Southampton	1989
2	102	Aus	MA Taylor	WI U/23	St Vincent	1990-91
2	101	AUS	MA TAYLOR	ENG	TRENT BRIDGE	1989
3	187*	AUS	GR MARSH	ENG	MCG	1990-91
3	166	Tas	MD Taylor	NSW	Syd	1987-88
3	155	Aus	DM Jones	Notts	Trent Bridge	1989
3	147	AUS	AR BORDER	ENG	SYDNEY	1990-91
3	139	AUS	AR BORDER	NZ	PERTH	1989-90
3	127	Aus	AR Border	Northants	Northampton	1989
3	127	Tas	RT Ponting	SA	Adelaide	1992-93
3	125	Tas	IR Beven	Vic	MCG	1983-84
3	118	Aus	SR Waugh	Hants	Southampton	1989
3	117	AUS	AR BORDER	IND	PERTH	1991-92
3	110*	AUS	AR BORDER	ENG	SYDNEY	1987-88
3	107	Aus	AR Border	Jam	Kingston	1990-91
3	107	AUS	DR MARTYN	NZ	AUCKLAND	1992-93
3	102	Tas	K Bradshaw	Vic	D'port	1984-85
3	100	AUS	ME WAUGH	WI	BRISBANE	1992-93
4	183	Aus	DM Jones	Kent	Canterbury	1989
4	174	Tas	BF Davison	Vic	TCA	1980-81
4	170	AUS	AR BORDER	WI	SYDNEY	1988-89
4	162	Aus	DM Wellham	Ess	Chelmsford	1985
4	117	AUS	GM RITCHIE	IND	ADELAIDE	1985-86
4	106	Aus	GM Ritchie	Northants	Northampton	1985

CENTURY PARTNERSHIPS IN FIRST-CLASS CRICKET continued

Wkt	P'ship	For	Partner	Versus*	Venue	Season
5	158	Tas	DA Smith	SA	D'port	1979–80
5	152	YAus	GM Ritchie	Zim	Harare	1982–83
5	137	Tas	RD Woolley	Qld	D'port	1981–82
5	133	Aus	DM Jones	Ess	Chelmsford	1989
5	126	Tas	RD Woolley	NSW	L'ton	1984–85
5	108*	Aus	WB Phillips	Som	Taunton	1985
5	104	Aus	AR Border	Worc	Worcester	1985
5	101	AUS	ME WAUGH	WI	KINGSTON	1990–91
6	150*	Aus	GRJ Matthews	Northants	Northampton	1985
6	147	Tas	SL Saunders	NSW	TCA	1985–86
6	114	Tas	RD Woolley	NSW	L'ton	1979–80
6	110	AUS	AR BORDER	ENG	ADELAIDE	1990–91
7	127	Tas	PI Faulkner	Vic	MCG	1983–84
7	125	YAus	MJ Bennett	Zim	Harare	1982–83

FIRST INNINGS VERSUS SECOND INNINGS IN ALL FIRST-CLASS CRICKET

	Inns	NO	HS	Runs	Aver.	100	50
1st Innings	205	11	227	9364	48.27	29	42
2nd Innings	144	21	184*	5139	41.78	13	25
Total	349	32	227	14503	45.75	42	67

Mode Of Dismissal

Mode	Test Matches		All First-class Matches	
	Number	Per cent	Number	Per cent
caught behind	18	15%	56	18%
caught & bowled	3	2%	8	3%
caught elsewhere	51	42%	140	44%
Total caught	72	59%	204	65%
bowled	21	17%	49	15%
lbw	20	17%	44	14%
run out	7	6%	13	4%
stumped	1	1%	7	2%
Total	121		317	

Bowlers To Dismiss D C Boon

152 different bowlers have dismissed Boon. Those to have dismissed him three or more times are:

10   MD Marshall

9   RJ Hadlee

6   RJ Bright, DE Malcolm, CJ McDermott, MG Hughes, CEL Ambrose

5   Kapil Dev, CA Walsh

4   JG Bracewell, TV Hohns, B Yardley, DR Gilbert, NA Foster, D Tazelaar, GC Small, PA Capes

3   W Prior, AL Mann, RG Holland, TG Hogan, AB Henschell, J Garner, JR Thomson, S Graf, BA Reid, GA Gooch, IT Botham, JE Emburey, RJ Shastri, PAJ de Freitas, CD Matthews, GR Dilley, M Prabhakar, Wasim Akram, BP Patterson, MR Whitney, PW Gladigau, IR Bishop, TBA May.

Dismissals By Bowler Type

Bowler type	Dismissals
Right-arm fast-medium	200
Left-arm fast-medium	34
Slow left arm	33
Left-arm wrist spin	2
Leg break/googly	20
Off-break	28

Test Record

	M	Inns	NO	HS	Runs	Aver.	100	50	Ca
1984–85 (WI/Aus)	3	5	0	51	132	26.40	0	1	2
1985 (Eng/Eng)	4	7	0	61	124	17.71	0	1	4
1985–86 (NZ/Aus)	3	6	0	81	175	29.16	0	2	1
1985–86 (Ind/Aus)	3	6	1	131	323	64.60	2	0	1
1985–86 (NZ/NZ)	3	5	1	70	176	44.00	0	2	2
1986–87 (Ind/Ind)	3	5	0	122	325	65.00	1	1	1
1986–87 (Eng/Aus)	4	8	0	103	144	18.00	1	0	1
1987–88 (NZ/Aus)	3	5	0	143	237	47.40	1	1	6
1987–88 (Eng/Aus)	1	2	1	184*	196	196.00	1	0	0
1987–88 (SL/Aus)	1	1	0	64	64	64.00	0	1	0
1988–89 (Pak/Pak)	3	6	0	43	117	19.50	0	0	10
1988–89 (WI/Aus)	5	10	1	149	397	44.11	1	2	9
1989 (Eng/Eng)	6	11	3	94	442	55.25	0	3	9
1989–90 (NZ/Aus)	1	1	0	200	200	200.00	1	0	1
1989–90 (SL/Aus)	2	4	0	41	67	16.75	0	0	1
1989–90 (Pak/Pak)	2	4	0	29	55	13.75	0	0	1
1989–90 (NZ/NZ)	1	2	0	12	12	6.00	0	0	0
1990–91 (Eng/Aus)	5	9	2	121	530	75.71	1	3	4

continues next page

TEST RECORD (continued)

	M	Inns	NO	HS	Runs	Aver.	100	50	Ca
1990–91 (WI/WI)	5	9	1	109*	266	33.25	1	1	1
1991–92 (Ind/Aus)	5	9	2	135	556	79.42	3	1	8
1992–93 (SL/SL)	3	6	0	68	161	26.83	0	1	3
1992–93 (WI/Aus)	5	10	2	111	490	61.25	1	3	5
1992–93 (NZ/NZ)	3	4	0	53	125	31.25	0	1	3
Total	74	135	14	200	5314	43.91	14	24	73

In Tests By Opponent

	M	Inns	NO	HS	Runs	Aver.	100	50	Ca
England	20	37	6	184*	1436	46.32	3	7	18
India	11	20	3	135	1204	70.82	6	2	10
New Zealand	14	23	1	200	925	42.05	2	6	13
Pakistan	5	10	0	43	172	17.20	0	0	11
Sri Lanka	6	11	0	68	292	26.54	0	2	4
West Indies	18	34	4	149	1285	42.83	3	7	17
	74	135	14	200	5314	43.91	14	24	73

TESTS BY REGION

	M	Inns	NO	HS	Runs	Aver.	100	50	Ca
In Aus	43	80	9	200	3566	50.22	12	14	40
In Eng	10	18	3	94	566	37.73	0	4	13
In Ind	3	5	0	122	325	65.00	1	1	1
In NZ	7	11	1	70	313	31.30	0	3	5
In Pak	3	6	0	43	117	19.50	0	0	10
In WI	5	9	1	109*	266	33.25	1	1	1
In SL	3	6	0	68	161	26.83	0	1	3
	74	135	14	200	5314	43.91	14	24	73

LIMITED OVERS INTERNATIONALS

Opp/Venue	M	Inns	NO	HS	Runs	Aver.	100	50	Ca
1983–84 (WI/Aus)	1	1	0	39	39	39.00	0	0	0
1984–85 (WI/Aus)	4	4	0	55	113	28.25	0	1	2
1984–85 (SL/Aus)	4	3	0	44	81	27.00	0	0	1
1985 (Eng/Eng)	3	3	0	45	70	23.33	0	0	0
1985–86 (NZ/Aus)	5	4	0	64	101	25.25	0	1	2
1985–86 (Ind/Aus)	7	7	0	83	317	45.28	0	3	0
1985–86 (NZ/NZ)	4	4	0	47	101	25.25	0	0	2
1985–86 (Pak/Sha)	1	1	0	44	44	44.00	0	0	0
1986–87 (Ind/Ind)	6	6	0	111	205	34.16	1	0	2
1986–87 (Eng/Aus)	1	1	0	1	1	1.00	0	0	0
1986–87 (Pak/Aus)	1	1	0	2	2	2.00	0	0	0
1986–87 (Pak/Sha)	1	1	0	71	71	71.00	0	1	0
1986–87 (Ind/Sha)	1	1	0	62	62	62.00	0	1	0
1986–87 (Eng/Sha)	1	1	0	73	73	73.00	0	1	0
1987–88 (Ind/Ind)	2	2	0	62	111	55.50	0	1	1

continues next page

LIMITED OVERS INTERNATIONALS (continued)

Opp/Venue	M	Inns	NO	HS	Runs	Aver.	100	50	Ca
1987–88 (Zim/Ind)	2	2	0	93	95	47.50	0	1	0
1987–88 (NZ/Ind)	2	2	0	87	101	50.50	0	1	1
1987–88 (Pak/Pak)	1	1	0	65	65	65.00	0	1	0
1987–88 (Eng/Ind)	1	1	0	75	75	75.00	0	1	0
1987–88 (SL/Aus)	4	4	0	122	194	48.50	1	1	2
1987–88 (NZ/Aus)	6	6	0	48	199	33.16	0	0	4
1987–88 (Eng/Aus)	1	1	0	33	33	33.00	0	0	0
1988–89 (Pak/Pak)	1	1	0	38	38	38.00	0	0	0
1988–89 (Pak/Aus)	4	4	0	45	107	26.75	0	0	1
1988–89 (WI/Aus)	7	7	0	71	157	22.42	0	1	3
1989 (Eng/Eng)	3	3	0	28	52	17.33	0	0	2
1989–90 (Eng/Ind)	1	1	0	0	0	0.00	0	0	0
1989–90 (WI/Ind)	1	1	0	1	1	1.00	0	0	0
1989–90 (Pak/Ind)	1	1	0	0	0	0.00	0	0	1
1989–90 (SL/Ind)	1	1	0	19	19	19.00	0	0	2
1989–90 (Ind/Ind)	1	1	0	49	49	49.00	0	0	1
1989–90 (SL/Aus)	2	2	1	49*	60	60.00	0	0	0
1989–90 (Pak/Aus)	1	1	0	39	39	39.00	0	0	0
1989–90 (Ind/NZ)	2	2	1	24*	46	46.00	0	0	0
1989–90 (NZ/NZ)	3	3	0	67	85	28.33	0	1	2
1989–90 (NZ/Sha)	1	1	1	92*	92	–	0	1	0
1989–90 (BD/Sha)	1	0	0	0	0	–	0	0	0
1989–90 (SL/Sha)	1	1	1	30*	30	–	0	0	0
1989–90 (Pak/Sha)	1	1	0	37	37	37.00	0	0	0
1990–91 (NZ/Aus)	6	6	2	40*	94	23.50	0	0	0
1990–91 (Eng/Aus)	4	4	0	42	94	23.50	0	0	1
1990–91 (WI/WI)	3	3	0	34	48	16.00	0	0	1
1991–92 (Ind/Aus)	6	6	2	102*	286	71.50	1	2	1
1991–92 (WI/Aus)	4	3	0	77	146	48.66	0	2	1

LIMITED OVERS INTERNATIONALS (continued)

Opp/Venue	M	Inns	NO	HS	Runs	Aver.	100	50	Ca
1991–92 (NZ/WC)	1	1	0	100	100	100.00	1	0	0
1991–92 (SAf/WC)	1	1	0	27	27	27.00	0	0	0
1991–92 (Ind/WC)	1	1	0	43	43	43.00	0	0	0
1991–92 (Eng/WC)	1	1	0	18	18	18.00	0	0	0
1991–92 (SL/WC)	1	1	1	27*	27	–	0	0	0
1991–92 (Pak/WC)	1	1	0	5	5	5.00	0	0	0
1991–92 (Zim/WC)	1	1	0	48	48	4 8.00	0	0	0
1991–92 (WI/WC)	1	1	0	100	100	100.00	1	0	0
1992–93 (SL/SL)	3	3	1	69*	104	52.00	0	1	1
1992–93 (WI/Aus)	6	6	0	19	56	9.33	0	0	0
1992–93 (Pak/Aus)	4	4	0	64	168	42.00	0	2	0
1992–93 (NZ/NZ)	4	4	0	55	99	24.75	0	1	1
	139	135	10	122	4428	35.42	5	25	35

LIMITED OVERS INTERNATIONALS BY COMPETITION
NC = Nehru Cup; WC = World Cup; Sha = Sharjah

Opp/Venue	M	Inns	NO	HS	Runs	Aver.	100	50	Ca
1983–84 (Aus)	1	1	0	39	39	39.00	0	0	0
1984–85(Aus)	8	7	0	55	194	27.71	0	1	3
1985(Eng)	3	3	0	45	70	23.33	0	0	0
1985–86(Aus)	12	11	0	83	418	38.00	0	4	2
1985–86(NZ)	4	4	0	47	101	25.25	0	0	2
1985–86(Sha)	1	1	0	44	44	44.00	0	0	0
1986–87(Ind)	6	6	0	111	205	34.16	1	0	2
1986–87(Aus)	2	2	0	2	3	1.50	0	0	0
1986–87(Sha)	3	3	0	73	206	68.66	0	3	0

continues next page

LIMITED OVERS INTERNATIONALS BY COMPETITION (continued)

Opp/Venue	M	Inns	NO	HS	Runs	Aver.	100	50	Ca
1987–88(WC)	8	8	0	93	447	55.87	0	5	2
1987–88(Aus)	11	11	0	122	426	38.72	1	1	6
1988–89(Pak)	1	1	0	38	38	38.00	0	0	0
1988–89(Aus)	11	11	0	71	264	24.00	0	1	4
1989(Eng)	3	3	0	28	52	17.33	0	0	2
1989–90(NC)	5	5	0	49	69	13.80	0	0	4
1989–90(Aus)	3	3	1	49*	99	49.50	0	0	0
1989–90(NZ)	5	5	1	67	131	32.75	0	1	2
1989–90(Sha)	4	3	2	92*	159	159.00	0	1	0
1990–91(Aus)	10	10	2	42	188	23.50	0	0	1
1990–91(WI)	3	3	0	34	48	16.00	0	0	1
1991–92(Aus)	10	9	2	102*	432	61.71	1	4	2
1991–92(WC)	8	8	1	100	368	52.57	2	0	0
1992–93(SL)	3	3	1	69*	104	52.00	0	1	1
1992–93(Aus)	10	10	0	64	224	22.40	0	2	0
1992–93(NZ)	4	4	0	55	99	24.75	0	1	1
	139	135	10	122	4428	35.42	5	25	35

LIMITED-OVER INTERNATIONALS BY SEASON

	M	Inns	NO	HS	Runs	Aver.	100	50	Ca
1983–84	1	1	0	39	39	39.00	0	0	0
1984–85	8	7	0	55	194	27.71	0	1	3
1985	3	3	0	45	70	23.33	0	0	0
1985–86	17	16	0	83	563	35.18	0	4	4
1986–87	11	11	0	111	414	37.63	1	3	2
1987–88	19	19	0	122	873	45.94	1	6	
1988–89	12	12	0	71	302	25.16	0	1	4
1989	3	3	0	28	52	17.33	0	0	2
1989–90	17	16	4	92*	458	38.16	0	2	6
1990–91	13	13	2	42	236	21.45	0	0	2
1991–92	18	17	3	102	800	57.14	3	4	2
1992–93	17	17	1	69*	427	26.68	0	4	2
	139	135	10	122	4428	35.42	5	25	35

LIMITED-OVER INTERNATIONALS BY OPPONENTS

	M	Inns	NO	HS	Runs	Aver.	100	50	Ca
Bangladesh	1	–	–	–	–	–	0	0	0
England	16	16	0	75	416	26.00	0	2	3
India	26	26	3	111	1119	48.65	2	7	5
New Zealand	32	31	3	100	972	34.71	1	5	12
Pakistan	17	17	0	71	576	33.88	0	4	2
South Africa	1	1	0	27	27	27.00	0	0	0
Sri Lanka	16	15	4	122	515	46.81	1	2	6
West Indies	27	26	0	100	660	25.38	1	4	7
Zimbabwe	3	3	0	93	143	47.66	0	1	0
	139	135	10	122	4428	35.42	5	25	35

Record For Tasmania In Limited-Overs Matches

	M	Inns	NO	HS	Runs	Aver.	100	50	Ca
Domestic Competition	34	32	1	94	1152	37.16	0	10	10
Versus Touring Teams	6	6	0	73	122	20.33	0	1	1
Total	40	38	1	94	1274	34.43	0	11	11

Bowling In First-Class Cricket

	Overs	Balls	Runs	Wkts	Aver.	5i	10m	BB
1979–80	6	36	37	1	37	0	0	1/19
1981–82	3	18	18	0	-	0	0	0/0
1984–85	3	18	12	1	12	0	0	1/12
1985 (Eng)	6	36	33	0	-	0	0	0/0
1985–86	0.4	4	2	0	-	0	0	0/0
1986–87 (Ind)	2	12	5	0	-	0	0	0/0
1986–87	37.10	223	124	1	124	0	0	1/18
1987–88	13.4	82	45	2	22.5	0	0	1/20
1988–89	7	42	26	0	-	0	0	0/0
1989 (Eng)	1	6	0	0	-	0	0	0/0
1992–93 (SL)	3	18	4	0	-	0	0	0/0
1992–93	16	96	57	1	57	0	0	1/56
1992–93	1	6	0	0	-	0	0	0/0
	99.30	597	363	6	60.5	0	0	1/12

D C Boon's First-Class Wickets

Date	Day	Batsman	Dismissal	Batsman's score
1/12/79	4	MF Kent	c RD Woolley	19
8/11/84	4	MD Taylor	c M Ray	118
3/11/86	3	CD Matthews	bowled	42
6/11/87	3	WS Andrews	bowled	72
1/2/88	4	SP George	lbw	1
3/11/92	4	NR Fielke	st MN Atkinson	74